PORTRAITS OF GREATNESS

General Editor
ENZO ORLANDI

Text by
GINO PUGNETTI

Translator
HELEN LAWRENCE

Published by
The Hamlyn Publishing Group Ltd
Hamlyn House, The Centre,
Feltham, Middlesex
First edition 1969
© Arnoldo Mondadori
Editore 1968
Translation © 1969 by
The Hamlyn Publishing Group Ltd.
Printed in Italy by
Arnoldo Mondadori, Verona

THE LIFE
AND
TIMES OF
MOZART

PAUL HAMLYN
London·New York·Sydney·Toronto

Below: view of Augsburg from the west, by Wayermann (Augsburg municipal museum). Situated at the confluence of the rivers Lech and Wertach, the city, of ancient Roman origin, has been the seat of a bishopric since the 6th century. Its period of greatest splendour was between the 15th and 16th centuries. It was then the centre of the famous Fugger bankers, who were Charles V's financiers amongst other things, and were still pre-eminent in banking and commercial activities in southern Germany. When the Mozarts established themselves there, Augsburg was still flourishing in every field. It cost a hundred florins to acquire citizenship, a sum laid out by the head of the family, Mozart's great-grandfather. Mozart's father, Johann Georg Leopold, known usually as Leopold, was born in Augsburg on November 14, 1719. He studied humanities at a Jesuit college in Salzburg and settled there in 1737. On the right: the house where Mozart's cheerful and placid mother was born.

THEY PAID TO BECOME CITIZENS OF AUGSBURG

Below: two portraits of Mozart's parents by unknown artists, today in the Salzburg Mozart Museum. The portrait of Leopold Mozart is of 1780; that of his wife, Anna Maria, was painted about 1775. They were married in 1747 when Mozart's father was 28. He had moved from Augsburg to Salzburg ten years before.

We find from their family tree that the Mozarts were of Swabian origin, although by the beginning of the 17th century they had already moved to Augsburg. The head of the family was David Mozart, Wolfgang Amadeus's great-grandfather. He was a master-mason, work which he must have found rewarding since he apprenticed three of his sons to it. The exception was Johann George, the fourth and youngest, who was destined to become a bookbinder. He sent his eldest son, Johann George Leopold, to study law and logic at Salzburg but the boy did not take to these studies. He had music in his blood and, attracted first by singing, then the organ, the violin and the pianoforte, he finally abandoned the university to devote himself entirely to the world which so fascinated him. Leopold Mozart is thus the first musician we find in the family. At St. Gilden, a little village on Lake Aber a few miles from Salzburg, he met a girl called Anna Maria Pertl, fell in love with her and married her in 1747. Their friends all agreed that they were the handsomest and most ideally suited couple ever seen. Anna Maria Pertl was as cheerful and optimistic as her husband was melancholy and pessimistic. Her goodness and lively nature were to enable her to overcome the difficulties she encountered during her life. Anna Maria Pertl's ancestors too are of interest: her great-grandfather, a coachman at the court, had through self-sacrifice and help from others sent his son to study law at Salzburg. To enable himself to live Wolf Nicolas Pertl got work at the theatre, first as a walk-on and then as a bass; he showed so much musical talent that he was appointed teacher of singing at the monastery church of St. Peter. Although he ended his life as a civil servant, this artistic interlude is enough to show that in Anna Maria's blood too there was a little of the musical instinct. It is said that boys take after their mothers and Wolfgang Amadeus is no exception. He greatly resembled his mother and inherited her characteristics of frankness, poetry and cheerfulness. But it was his father who ruled the household. Leopold Mozart was a kindly husband and father but a very authoritarian one. It was he who selected everything which came into the house: food, servants, friends—all needed his approval.

5

Salzburg, which came under Austrian rule only in 1816, was in Mozart's time a city of 10,000 inhabitants. Its artistic tradition, especially in music, was long established. The first presentation of an Italian opera in Germany took place here.
The Felsentheater had been finished in 1693, with 23 boxes and

3 galleries. Many were the presentations which took place, like the forerunners of today's festival.
Below: the font used for Wolfgang's baptism.
Bottom: the room where he was born as it is today. On the wall hangs a portrait of his father, Leopold Mozart.

A DIET OF WATER FOR THE NEWLYBORN MOZART

Of 7 children born to Anna and Leopold Mozart, only 2 survived: Nannerl, who was born on July 30, 1751 and was christened Maria Anna, and Wolfgang, whose birthday was January 27, 1756. Actually, in the baptismal register his name appears as Johann Chrysostomus Wolfgang Theophilus, Theophilus later being altered to the simpler and more harmonious equivalent, Amadeus. 18th-century standards of hygiene or medical knowledge were not of the highest and it is not, therefore, surprising that the infant mortality rate sadly affected the Mozart family too. If Wolfgang, the last to arrive, did not follow his prematurely deceased brothers, it was despite the doctors of the "enlightened" 18th century, whose prescription for his diet was plain water. The room in which he was born was in a modest house in Getreidestrasse (Wheat Lane). The birth nearly cost his mother's life and consequently there was no mother's milk for Wolfgang, only water. The little boy did not begin to walk until he was 3 years old, but his first steps were, so to speak, taken in the direction of the pianoforte from which he drew his first sounds. And the piano was his first and greatest toy. The Mozarts lived on the third floor of a small 15th-century house acquired by the merchant Hagenauer in 1713: there were 3 big rooms, one smaller one and a kitchen. Nannerl had already revealed her musical talent to her father and soon made rapid progress in her studies. A deep friendship free of any jealousy bound the two children from their first years. Nannerl, who had the same sweet, sensitive nature as her brother, was always the favourite object of his childish jokes, but she tolerated them cheerfully. In Wolfgang too Leopold soon discovered a precocious natural musical talent. Astounded more every day by the child's apparent gifts, he began to watch him with increasing interest: he gave him bells, a violin, and even lids and saucepans, on all of which Wolfgang produced the most varied and original sounds. At the age of 3 he could repeat a melody played to him by his father, at 4 reproduce it at the piano and at 5 learn a minuet and trio by heart in half an hour. Leopold began to have great hopes for his son, but for the time being he kept silent about them.

The Austrian poet, Hugo von Hofmansthal, has described in a few lines the relationship between Mozart and the city of his birth. "Salzburg", he wrote, "an ancient city within its surrounding wall, symbolizes at once the new and the old, the magnificence of baroque and the eternal grace of the rustic. Mozart is the expression of all this. There is not a lovelier place in all central Europe and Mozart had to be born there."
Left: Löchelplatz, Salzburg, with the house where Mozart was born in the centre, (Salzburg Museum).
Below: an 18th-century print of the town and the citadel showing the mountain background (today in the Mozarteum, Salzburg).

*Right : the inner courtyard of the
house where Mozart was born.
The windows of the apartments
looked out into a courtyard of
flower-covered balconies, dominated
by the bell-tower of St. Peter
(top of the photograph). The church
of St. Peter was also the church
of Salzburg University, where
Leopold had studied.*

*Above : the Hagenauers, Maria
Teresa and Johann Lorenz, owners
of the house where Mozart was
born (the Mozarteum, Salzburg).
All the Hagenauers were friends of
the Mozart family. Hagenauer was
a well-to-do wholesale merchant.
It was he who provided the
necessary money for the various
journeys which Leopold made with
his son across Europe.*

SALZBURG, A BEAUTIFUL AND GAY CITY

The cult of the memory of its great son is one of the most dominant aspects of Salzburg life. Its manifestations are many: the Mozarteum, the birthplace museum about young Mozart, the little train which takes you to Gaisberg, to the Academic Society and the "Weeks" in January. All this culminates in the famous summer festival to which music lovers and tourists in search of cultural diversion come each year from all over the world. Below: a characteristic street of old Salzburg, the Street of Signs. Bottom: two views of the park of Leopoldskrom House, the home of the Prince-Archbishop Firmian, Leopold Mozart's patron.

Salzburg, a university city and seat of the Prince-Archbishop who was primate of Germany, was not just a charming town set in the verdant hills by the banks of the Salzach; it was above all a gay, lively town which loved the arts. Fortunately for Mozart the reigning prince of Salzburg at the time when he was born was Archbishop Sigismund III von Schrattenbach, a noble, benevolent and pious man under whose enlightened and tolerant rule honest devotion to the Catholic church flourished. Sigismund III's predecessors had shown no lack of good taste in their attempts to create new visual effects in Salzburg. They had greatly improved and beautified the town by demolishing and rebuilding the facades of old houses and re-arranging entire areas with new streets and squares. If for aesthetic reasons it had appeared necessary, they had simply elevated the facades of some of the palaces so that they were out of proportion to the rest of the building behind. In short, they created an architectural environment which no other city could rival, beautifying and embellishing every corner. It was in this beautiful and gracious town that Mozart took his first walks accompanied by his mother; he saw elegant streets, and enchanting palaces. The sky was blue, the countryside peaceful and all was perfect harmony. In the middle ages the archbishop of Salzburg, which was then an ancient seat of learning, had secured the first place in the hierarchy of German ecclesiastical states. The princes of the Church were rich, feared and adulated. Their home was the Hohensalzburg Castle, typically gloomy and massive, built with riches acquired from the gold and silver mines of the Tauri Mountains and from salt, the other mineral wealth from which Salzburg derives its name. By the beginning of the 15th century interest in music was already increasing among the citizens of Salzburg and with the passing of the centuries was pursued and widened, so that by the 18th century theatres were always full, inns resounded with singing day and night and the nobility frequently made music in their houses. And like the temperament of the Salzburg people, who put their amusements above all else, it was always gay music. Wolfgang grew up, then, in a serene, happy, enlightened and musical town.

Right: an oil portrait of Sigismund von Schrattenbach, who was Prince-Archbishop of Salzburg from 1753 to 1772 (Salzburg Municipal Museum). This great prelate was a patron of the arts and the theatre and friend to the Mozarts. Mozart's father held the post of vice-Kappellmeister in his chapel choir. The unsigned portrait in pencil next to it can be found in the Salzburg Mozarteum and is an exact likeness of Leopold Mozart in 1762. Below: Salzburg cathedral square in an 18th-century painting in the city museum. The square was dominated by the baroque facade of the church, plainly seen here. The archbishop's palace also faced onto the square.

HIS FATHER WAS HIS FIRST TEACHER

Below: a view of the Robining family's country house, Robinghof, near Salzburg, where the Mozarts often went on excursions. Luisa, especially, was a true friend to Wolfgang. Bottom: the title-page and frontispiece (with a portrait of the author) of the noted work on the study of the violin published by Leopold Mozart in Augsburg in 1756. In addition to a study of the technique of the instrument, the author advocates certain ideals and concepts revealing him as a true man of his time, believing in the principles of the enlightenment. He also expected the musician to be a "good Christian, a humanist and an honest man".

Having left the university without completing his studies, to take up a musical career, Leopold Mozart found life neither easy nor brilliant. He entered the service of the Count of Thurn as "groom of the chamber with duties as musician". Later he became fourth violinist in the Prince Archbishop's orchestra. Finally he became court composer and vice-Kapell-meister. However in 1756, the year his son Wolfgang was born, Leopold's reputation in the musical world was widely increased when his book *A Thorough Violin School Essay'd* was published in Augsburg by the printer Lotter. Its fame spread as far afield as France, Holland and Italy and the critic Zelter, a friend of Goethe, predicted that the work would be used as long as the violin was played; he added that it was written in the best German, with discernment and intelligence, and that although the musical examples were inspired by the Tartini school they were excellently chosen and applied without pedantry. Wolfgang Amadeus Mozart thus had for his first teacher not a drunkard father as did Beethoven, but a serious and esteemed musician who loved and guided him throughout nearly his whole life. Leopold no doubt hoped that Wolfgang would succeed where he had failed. Wolfgang was in every sense his father's creation: at the age of 5 he learnt to improvise at the harpsichord and played the violin with perfect intonation. Like other children, he was gay and impetuous even to excess, but as soon as he sat at the piano his face took on a serious expression which contrasted with his childishness and his small, delicate hands. Quite a number of people, apart from his own parents, showed concern for this unusually gifted boy who seemed in his quiet and pensive moments almost to give some hint of a short, sad life. To play was the greatest amusement of the day. He listened to his father's lessons and studied with humility and determination. At 6 he composed his first minuet, and ran to show it to his father. Smilingly Leopold began to read that music traced by the childish hand: but soon the smile gave place to tears. He expected the childish ingenuity of the little composition, but he also observed that every note had its correct value and that an unexpected beauty emanated from the music while the flow of ideas was uninterrupted.

THE CHILD PRODIGY DOES NOT LIKE TO GIVE DISPLAYS

The miniature, below left, portrays Mozart and his sister as children. Next to it is a drawing in silk and parchment with a rhyme, attributed to Leopold Mozart. The page below is from a music copy-book, which belonged to Wolfgang's sister and is his first piece written at the age of 6—the minuet in G Major.

Leopold's first enthusiasm over the wonderful musical talents of his little son soon developed into a conviction of a mission in life: to educate Wolfgang, to teach, form and urge him to become a great pianist and composer. Soon the day came when he took him to play at the court of the prince-archbishop; they listened with evident enjoyment and then called to him and asked him various questions, which he answered with a self-possession which quite charmed them; such adjectives as "phenomenal" and "prodigious" were used of him. His father realised that others would also listen and applaud and perhaps lend him financial aid. Wolfgang did not really like this kind of display in front of strangers, and he could see that they were more interested in him than in the music. Once a friend of his father pretended to be a theatrical agent disposed to engage him after a private hearing. However, he did not expect such genius in a child, and on hearing Wolfgang play the enthusiastic listener was unable to contain his wonder and burst into comments of praise which disturbed the child's concentra-

tion. All at once he became impatient, stopped playing and left the room, refusing to return to the keyboard. One can attempt to draw from this some conclusions about Wolfgang's character: he was enthusiastic, impulsive and like most children of his age given to spontaneous laughter; but he could change suddenly and become obstinate or sad. It was his mother who would bring him back to a happy mood again. His father required a seriousness and regularity in his studies which were almost excessive; the carefree child suddenly became adult when placed at the keyboard. Soon young Mozart's prowess had been admired by everyone in the small circle at Salzburg and Leopold became ambitious to make his son's genius known further afield. He decided, therefore, to organize a tour for Wolfgang. The first stage of this concert tour of 1762 was Munich, where they arrived just at the time of the carnival. Wolfgang was 6 and his sister 11. They were to spend much of their childhood travelling, in lumbering coaches, from city to city.

Nannerl was 5 years' older than her brother Wolfgang. She was a good pianist and also had a pretty voice. She has recorded for us an important story about Mozart as a little boy: " As soon as he began to dedicate himself to music, all his senses were as good as dead to every other occupation. Even his games with toys had to be accompanied by music if they were to interest him. When we carried our toys from one room to another, whoever was empty-handed had to sing or fiddle a march."
Left: the kitchen of the house where Mozart was born, with the original oven. Below: the old town market about 1750 (a coloured print).

The concert that the six-year old
Mozart gave for the Empress
Maria Theresa at Schönbrunn is
recorded in the palace itself in a
large painting, by an unknown
artist, of which we show a detail
above. In it little Wolfgang is shown
seated between his first patron
Sigismund von Schrattenbach,
prince-archbishop of Salzburg, and
his father Leopold, his teacher.
Right: the entrance to the
Schönbrunn Castle.

WOLFGANG MEETS THE EMPRESS

On their first trip to Munich Wolfgang and Nannerl played duets together, and so great was their success that they were detained there for three more weeks and gave many concerts. People were greatly impressed and after the performances would surround Wolfgang, ask him questions and give him presents. Despite Leopold's perfect organization, their financial gain was not great. However, Mozart's father was wise: he did not worry about the meagre compensation of the present, but thought above all of future arrangements for his son. Leopold considered these first concerts and the publicity they generated to be good experience which would bear fruit later. In September 1762 the Mozart family travelled on to Vienna, staying there until the following January. Many people did not hide their criticism of Leopold Mozart. They felt that such extensive voyages across Europe and the ensuing exhibitions were unsuitable for this young prodigy. But Leopold did not allow himself to be troubled by this disapproval; the journey from Munich to Vienna was made in short stages and the two little pianists were able to keep up their practising on a dummy keyboard which their impresario father had brought with their luggage. Thus in every city between Munich and Vienna Wolfgang and Nannerl gave concerts and were always greatly admired. If there was no hall available Wolfgang played the organ of some crowded church, where the success was repeated. At last the Mozarts arrived in Vienna. The child was taken to admire the palaces and to visit the Prater; the Viennese aristocracy seemed to vie with each other to invite the Mozart children to give concerts. Before long Wolfgang was even invited to Schönbrunn Castle, the baroque palace which was the home of the Empress Maria Theresa.

Above the text: The Prater, Vienna, an engraving in the Oest Nationalbibliotek, Vienna. Top: Munich in the 18th century (Bertarelli Collection, Milan). Above: a room in the 18th century manner in the prince-archbishop of Salzburg's palace. On the wall is a portrait of Sigismund von Schrattenbach. It was in his presence that Mozart the child prodigy made his first public appearance. Schrattenbach was greatly mourned, especially by Mozart to whom he always showed paternal benevolence. His relationship with his successor, Colloredo, was much more discordant. While one remembers the former for his love of the arts, the latter owes his notoriety to his rude manner and the lack of intelligence in his dealings with Mozart. Hieronymus Joseph, Count of Colloredo, was born in 1732 and died in 1812.

WOLFGANG AND NANNERL TRIUMPH IN VIENNA

The eyes of Europe were turned on Vienna in the second half of the 18th century. Maria Theresa is regarded as having been an exemplary queen, wise and cultured: she it was who restored the country after the ravages of wars and initiated a period of ordered and enlightened administration which was to make Austria a model state. Under Maria Theresa life in Vienna reached a level of artistic achievement unequalled by any other capital and the intellectual activity influenced and elevated the social life. Every family took part in cultural activities: music-dramas, concerts and masked balls were held in both homes and theatres. Maria Theresa herself was a pupil of the composer Hasse and had a pleasant singing voice; her daughter played the piano and her son—the future emperor Joseph II—was a proficient cellist. This background explains the immediate interest of Maria Theresa in little Wolfgang and the consequent invitation to play at court. When the Mozart children appeared in the great concert hall at Schönbrunn, they were greeted by long and enthusiastic applause. After having played some duets with his sister, Wolfgang enjoyed himself playing with the little princes and princesses in the rooms and along the corridors of the huge palace. He jumped on the empress's lap and kissed her, at which she laughed and hugged him affectionately. Once, when Wolfgang slipped on one of the highly polished floors, it was the little archduchess Marie Antoinette, the future queen of France who was destined to be guillotined, who helped him to his feet. Mozart looked at her, smiling, and said: "You are very kind; when I am grown-up, I shall marry you." During this stay, Leopold Mozart noted in his diary: "Our concerts are all booked in advance by the nobility. Everyone is enamoured of my children. I have not yet met anyone who, after hearing Mozart, does not say 'incredible'!" However Nannerl and Wolfgang's triumphs were interrupted by an attack of scarlet fever with which the little boy fell ill. Vienna was interested in their health, but the citizens prudently kept well away. Meanwhile, the permit given by the archbishop to his "musicus" Leopold had expired, and thus, at the beginning of January, 1763, the whole family returned once again to Salzburg.

Above: Wolfgang and Marianna in their court costumes given to them by the Empress Maria Theresa (Mozarteum, Salzburg). When the two children played at the Schönbrunn Castle, Nannerl was dressed like a little lady, with a corset round her waist, wide embroidered skirts, necklace and earrings. Wolfgang wore white silk stockings, orange velvet breeches, a close-fitting lilac-coloured jacket and an embroidered waistcoat, with lace at collar and cuffs. The picture on the left by E. Ender shows Leopold Mozart presenting his son to the Imperial family. Two concerts were given at Schönbrunn.

TOURING EUROPE LIKE A SIDESHOW

The journeys, fabulous receptions and easy successes did not change Wolfgang's personality; he was still unaffected, respectful, faithful to those closest to him. His best sentiments were revealed in music. One evening when a few friends had met to play through a quartet at Mozart's home one of them was late, and Wolfgang asked if he could play the part instead. To his father his request seemed an absurd caprice, and he scolded the child, who burst into tears. Schachtner, an old friend of the family, intervened and persuaded Leopold to let the child play, just for a joke. But it was not a joke at all: Wolfgang sight-read the whole second violin part quite correctly. While Wolfgang leapt to his feet crying joyfully: "Now I shall be able to play the violin too! The violin!", Leopold remained, head bowed and his eyes filled with tears. Now Leopold began to plan a new and even more ambitious tour to show off his son's ever more brilliant and precious talents. So six months after their return from Vienna they set off again, this time for Paris and London. The journey along the bumpy roads was made in short stages and between June and November

Above left: a portrait of Mozart aged seven done during his first visit to Paris (Paris, National Library). Above, across the two pages: Frankfurt from the south west, an engraving by Reinheimer, from J. F. Morgenstern (Goethe Museum, Dusseldorf). The gold ring (left) with a vase of flowers of emeralds, diamonds, rubies and a little turquoise, was a gift to Mozart from the prince-bishop of Augsburg in 1763 on the occasion of one of his concerts there.
The prints to the left show views of Ulm, Brussels and Vienna in the 18th century.
The print on the right shows the Hôtel de Beauvais, where the Mozarts stayed on their arrival in Paris (Bibliothèque Nationale, Paris).

1763 the two children played at Augsburg, Ulm, Cologne and Brussels, always with great success. This announcement, which appeared in a German newspaper in 1763, gives some idea of the atmosphere in which they lived during these trips: "The very last concert! The 7-year-old will not only play the harpsichord, but also a violin concerto; he will accompany symphonies on the clavier and, completely covering the keyboard with a cloth, will play with the same sureness as though he could actually see the keys. He will recognize from a distance any notes sounded for him on the piano or on any other instrument including bells, glasses and clocks. Lastly, he will improvise on the pianoforte or the organ for however long is desired. Admission: a half taler per person." There is a note of vulgarity in such an announcement, reminiscent more of a circus act than a musical genius. Present at one of these concerts was a 14-year-old boy by the name of Wolfgang Goethe. Many years later, the great poet recalled with emotion the appearance of the little musician with the pale, smiling face.

AT VERSAILLES BEFORE MADAME DE POMPADOUR

In November 1763 the Mozarts' little procession made its way into Paris. To Wolfgang, the city seemed like an enchanted town: he was amazed by the busy streets, the friendliness of the people and the sheer joy of life which pervaded the atmosphere. Although from certain quarters critical voices were raised, King Louis XV enjoyed the respect of the mass of the French people, who still felt for their king an almost religious awe. The turmoil of the revolution was still to come. Paris and the rich Parisians still had plenty of time to interest themselves in little Mozart whose fame had already reached the town months ago. So great was their welcome and the interest shown in the little pianist that the Mozart family prolonged their stay in Paris from November 1763 to April 1764. They were warmly welcomed by the Baroness Arco, wife of the Bavarian ambassador and a fellow-citizen of Salzburg, at whose home, the Hôtel de Beauvais, they stayed. Their friend, the writer and critic Baron Melchior von Grimm, who had important contacts, looked after their interests and it was through him that Wolfgang and his sister were invited to play on New Year's Day at Versailles before Madame de Pompadour; a charming evening full of compliments, smiles and applause. They were also invited to dinner and were admitted to the *grand couvert*. Wolfgang sat next to the Queen and amused her greatly, chattering away, kissing her hands and eating from the dishes which she graciously handed him. The Queen spoke excellent German and translated everything the little pianist said for Louis XV, who knew none. It was in Paris that Wolfgang wrote some of his earliest compositions—four sonatas for harpsichord and violin which he dedicated to the king's second daughter, Princess Victoria.

On April 2, 1764, during Mozart's stay in Paris, the artist dilettante, Louis Carrogis de Carmontelle, painted a portrait of Wolfgang seated at the piano. The version we show you here (on the facing page) is in the British Museum. Leopold Mozart noted of it: " Wolfgang is at the piano, I stand behind him playing the violin and Marianna, leaning against the piano, holds some music as if she were singing." Above the text: a

view of Versailles (a print in the Bibliothèque Nationale, Paris). Top: a portrait of Madame de Pompadour, mistress of Louis XV, by Boucher (private collection). Above: Louis XV by F. H. Drouain (left) and Louis Philippe, Duke of Chartres, the future Philippe-Egalité of revolutionary times. He was 16 at the time Mozart was in Paris and his tutor was Carmontelle who was at one time a friend of Grimm.

LONDON, CITY OF HANDEL

In the spring of 1764, the Mozarts exchanged the French court for the English court. England was fast becoming the greatest colonial power in the world: five years ago she had conquered Quebec and Montreal and now all Canada was British. Soon East India was to come under her rule, while James Cook would discover the fertile coast of eastern Australia and occupy it in the name of the British sovereign. The same period saw the beginnings of the industrial revolution, with its great technical achievements such as the steam engine and the spinning machine. But while commerce and colonization flourished there was a diminution in the importance of English music. When the Mozarts reached the English capital, young George III had been on the throne for only four years. Since Henry Purcell, the last great national composer, had died in 1695, the English had had to "import" music; but they knew well how to choose, appreciate and pay foreign musicians. Handel, who had lived in England for half a century and had achieved wide fame during his brilliant career, had died five years earlier. London's musical life was now dominated by a large group of Italian and German composers. The opera at the King's Theatre in the Haymarket was also Italian, although English national opera, which lagged far behind the Italian, received new impetus in the 1760s through the work of Thomas Arne and Samuel Arnold at Covent Garden. The principal composer for the King's Theatre was Johann Sebastian Bach's younger son, Johann Christian. Among London's musical organizations was the Society of St. Cecilia which gave performances of old music. The most important musical enterprise, however, was the series of concerts presented by J. C. Bach in partnership with Karl Friedrich Abel. In London, therefore, Mozart was able to hear the operas of Piccini, Handel's oratorios and the symphonies of Bach; he discovered a new instrument, the clarinet, for which he wrote—at the end of his life—the beautiful concerto, K.622. Wolfgang, who never felt much liking for the French, always found himself at ease with the English. Several times he thought of settling in England, and although politics interested him little he sided with that country in any difficult situation, for all the world like a genuine Englishman.

Above: London in a water colour by Canaletto (British Museum, London). Below: King George III and his consort, Charlotte of Mecklenburg-Strelitz. Only four days after their arrival in London, the Mozarts had the honour of being heard at Court where they played again on 19 May and 25 October, 1764. " At all the courts we have been received with extraordinary courtesy, but our reception here surpasses all the others", Leopold Mozart wrote from London.

Left: a view of St. James Park in front of Buckingham House by E. Dayes (Victoria and Albert Museum, London). Below: Buckingham House, later Buckingham Palace, an 18th-century print (British Museum).

The child prodigy's stay in London, or more correctly, in England, was amongst the longest on his tour of 1762–8; it lasted, in fact, from summer 1764 to summer 1765. It was also one of the most profitable with regard to the education of the young boy. Handel's music, although already less fashionable, made a great impression on him. Most important of all was the meeting with Johann Sebastian Bach's youngest son. *Right: the King's Italian Opera House, Haymarket, which Mozart visited while he was in London (John Soane Museum). Below: a musical evening on the Thames in a painting by Zoffany (The Royal Academy of Art, London).*

GEORGE III STOPS TO GREET THEM

Wolfgang dedicated Six Clavichord and Violin sonatas, written in London, to Queen Charlotte. Bernard Gavoty wrote of these: "whatever you do it is impossible to imagine something different or better than that which is promised". Below the composer's name on the title page, it is precisely stated in French that he is "agé de huit ans", adding that it contains his third opus ("Oeuvre 111"). Below: the concert hall at Vauxhall Gardens in 1755, a coloured print by A. Wade (British Museum, London) and (bottom) a view of London showing St. Paul's Cathedral and the river, acquired while there by Leopold Mozart (Salzburg Mozarteum).

In contrast to Paris and Vienna, the children were summoned to court almost at once. Young King George III and his German wife were enthusiastic musical amateurs. The king delighted in Handel's music and regularly attended the concerts given by the Society of St. Cecilia as well as those given by the court chapel; the queen sang and played the clavier— "quite tolerably for a queen", according to Haydn— and attended the opera once a week. On April 27, 1764, Wolfgang and Nannerl gave their first concert at court, between 6 and 9 in the evening. Their reception was extremely cordial and the graciousness of the royal couple reconciled Leopold to the meagre fee of 24 guineas. Eight days after this concert, the Mozarts were strolling in St. James's Park when they chanced to meet the royal coach: the king opened the window and smilingly greeted them, nodding and waving his hand, particularly to little Mozart. Less than a month later, on May 19, the children gave a second concert at court during which the king amused himself by placing on the music stand scores by Wagenseil, Handel and J. C. Bach, but Wolfgang, unperturbed, read them all at sight. He also played most impressively on the king's organ, accompanied the queen as she sang an aria, and finally improvised the most beautiful melody on the bass of a Handel aria. "What he knew when we departed from Salzburg", wrote his father, "is a mere shadow of what he now knows. It surpasses all imagination." After the interest shown at court, the curiosity of the public was aroused and Leopold began to organize some public concerts. After some postponements due to Wolfgang being ill, the first concert took place on June 5, in the large exhibition hall of the Academy of Painters in Spring Gardens, near Charing Cross. Besides Wolfgang and Nannerl, the singers Cremoni and Quilici and the violinist Cirri also took part in this "grand vocal and instrumental concert" which was a sensational success, financially as well as musically, and earned for the family some hundreds of guineas. Wolfgang was also asked to play at a charity concert given in the Rotunda at Raneleagh Gardens in aid of a new hospital, after which they went to the popular resort of Tunbridge Wells, south of London, for a short stay, and then removed to Chelsea.

DELAYED BY ILLNESS

The Mozarts' long, tiring journey home from London was interrupted by concerts and illnesses. On August 1, at Lille, father and son had to take to their beds for a month. "Half well and half ill", as Leopold noted, they travelled on to Ghent and Antwerp, where Wolfgang played on the famous cathedral organ. Then by carriage through Moerdijk and Rotterdam to the Hague, which they reached on the evening of September 11. The Princess of Nassau-Weilburg had persuaded them to visit Holland and warmly welcomed the Mozart children who were to play at an orchestral concert which had been arranged for them for the 30th. Nannerl did not feel well when they arrived at the Hague and in fact she had intestinal typhoid. She became so ill that the doctors feared for her life, and on October 21 the Holy Sacrament was administered to her; however, her strong constitution was miraculously able to withstand the crisis. Then Wolfgang too caught the fever, and according to the diary "was reduced to a most pitiable state, seeming to have nothing left but skin and bone". When the Mozart children finally recovered, they were able to give some more concerts at the Hague, Amsterdam and Utrecht. Wolfgang dedicated six sonatas he composed there to the

princess. Then they proceeded via Brussels to Paris which they reached on the evening of May 10, 1766. They played at court and at various other salons including that of the prince of Conti, but the public did not seem as enthusiastic as before. However, one new acquaintance which gave Leopold great satisfaction and made a great impression on Mozart was Prince Karl Wilhelm Friedrich, heir to the Duchy of Brunswick, hero of the Seven Years' War and a sensitive and cultured musician. On hearing Mozart, he said amazed: "Many Kappelmeister will die without ever having learned what this child knows." The prince of Conti was a member of a distant branch of the Bourbon family (the Bourbon Condé line). An oil painting by the artist Ollivier, today in the Louvre, immortalizes a concert Wolfgang gave at their fabulous palace in Paris.

Michel Barthélemy Olliver's painting of 1776 records faithfully an "English tea" in the salon of 4 mirrors at the Temple, the home of the prince of Condé (portrayed on the left). Little Wolfgang is seated on a large chair at the harpsichord. Standing beside him is the singer Jelyotte, accompanying himself on the guitar. Amongst the Prince's guests are many famous names: the countess of Egmont and the count of Chabon-Rohann, to name but two.

Although there are many pictures in existence concerned with Mozart's life and times, we have few actually of him. One of them is this portrait (below) painted in London between 1764 and 1765 by the artist Zoffany. Wolfgang was aged about eight at this time and the painter—with obvious intention—shows him holding a nest containing some nightingales' eggs. Johann (or John) Zoffany was born in Frankfurt in 1733 and settled in England in 1761. There he remained almost without interruption until his death in 1810. He was a society painter whose pictures are considered to be an accurate and lively record of the fashions of his time.

J. C. BACH BECOMES A CLOSE FRIEND

It was in London that Wolfgang had made an important friend. In the middle of their successful London season Leopold had contracted a severe cold and was advised by the doctors to withdraw with his family to Chelsea, then a little village on the outskirts of London. It was July and it was to this illness, which obliged the Mozarts to stay there for seven weeks, that we owe some charming compositions: the house had to be kept very still and the clavier silent, and Leopold was in no condition to give his usual lessons. The 9-year-old composer was left largely to himself and composed away gaily; he wrote his first three symphonies, K 16, 17 and 19. In them we see just how much he was influenced by his father, who probably polished the works afterwards, but also from some clumsy turns in composition, discarded in his note-books, we realise how much work and learning even such a genius as this needed to do. In these early compositions one can naturally detect the influence of other musicians, but above all of J. C. Bach. Despite the great difference in their ages, Bach became a great friend and adviser of Wolfgang. J. C. Bach had studied in Italy with the famous Padre Martini of Bologna and was organist of Milan Cathedral for two years before being called to London. Wolfgang would sit on Bach's lap while they played the clavier together, or discussed new instruments or styles or accompaniments. This friendship perhaps created one of the strongest influences, both personal and artistic, that can be found in Mozart's life. London was a bigger city than Paris and Mozart could go often to the theatre where he saw beautiful productions of Italian operas sung by the best singers, amongst whom the male sopranos Giusto Fernando Tenducci of Siena and the Florentine Giovanni Manzuoli became his great friends; they taught him how to use the voice, especially for opera, and aroused in him the interest which was to lead to some of his great masterpieces. Leaving the countryside of Chelsea the Mozarts returned to London, but various political disturbances and the worsening symptoms of the King's mental illness rendered it an inappropriate time for giving concerts. On July 24, 1765 therefore, the family left London to cross the Channel and continue their concert tour on the continent.

Left to right: the singers Manzuoli and Tenducci and J. Christian Bach. Giusto Fernando Tenducci was, like Manzuoli, a famous castrato. This did not stop him having many amorous adventures however. He eventually married and was even tried for adultery. Apart from being a brilliant singer, he was a noted composer.

Above: the gardens and the Rotunda at Ranaleagh House in which Mozart gave a concert, from a coloured print of about 1750 (the British Museum, London). Left: a view of Chelsea, about 1750 when it was still a village, in an engraving by Z. Boremann (British Museum). In July, 1764, when Leopold fell gravely ill, he moved to Chelsea where he stayed with his family for a period of seven weeks, convalescing, at the house of a Dr. Randal.

ON THEIR HOMEWARD JOURNEY, A CONCERT AT EVERY TOWN

One is astonished, when looking at a map, to see the tiring and extraordinary itinerary of the Mozart family's journey across Europe. A journey which today takes half-an-hour by aeroplane took several days at the beginning of the 18th century. Paris was linked with 43 smaller towns by public coaches pulled by four or six horses and capable of carrying eight people. Some routes had daily services, others weekly or fortnightly. The journey from Paris to Dijon took eight or nine days, and many vehicles arrived at their destination damaged by accidents on the bumpy roads. The first stagecoach in the world came into service in 1737 and in Mozart's time their average speed was still only about eight miles per hour and their maximum speed was 15 to 16 miles. In 1775, night journeys were introduced to save time. But the Mozarts were used to continual travelling and all the difficulties which beset them were repaid by the enthusiasm which greeted them and by their earnings. Leaving Paris on July 9 they proceeded to Dijon where the last entries in the travel journal were made. The notebook was full and we do not know whether the meticulous Leopold began a second notebook which has been lost, or whether he dispensed with taking notes during the last four months of the tour. After a fortnight in Dijon, where they had been invited by the Prince de Condé to perform at the Assembly of the Estates of Burgundy, and a month in Lyons, they arrived in Geneva. Here they were not very far from the philosopher Voltaire at the nearby Chateau de Ferney, but Voltaire was too ill at the time to receive visitors, and in any case the Catholic family were antagonistic towards the old doubter. Afterwards he wrote to Madame d'Epinay: "As you know, I live at a distance of eight miles from Geneva. I never go out and I was very ill when this phenomenon shone upon the black horizon of Geneva. Now it is gone and to my great regret without my having seen it." from Geneva they went on to Lausanne, Berne and Zurich and thence to Munich via Schaffhausen, Ulm, Dillinger and Augsburg, all during weeks of intense music making. Wolfgang suffered an attack of rheumatic fever before they finally returned to Salzburg laden with presents and happy memories. Mozart was now ten years old.

Above from the top: views of the Port of Amsterdam (Bertarelli Collection, Milan), Geneva (coloured print, Oest. National bibliothek, Vienna) and Lausanne (Bertarelli collection, Milan), all of which were visited by Mozart during his tour. Left: a portrait of Gluck, painted by Quendy (Opera Museum, Paris).

THEY ALREADY FEARED HIM AS A RIVAL

Archbishop Sigismund had generously allowed Leopold leave of absence between 1763–6 to take his son on the tour and was delighted at the enthusiastic reports which reached him about his "musicus". This kind and indulgent man looked with affection on little Mozart. Now ten years old, he was respectful and pious, although he could also be gay and mischievous. During the Mozarts' absence Michael Haydn, the younger brother of the great Joseph Haydn, had come to settle in Salzburg. Also a composer, but better known as a teacher, he became a great friend of the Mozarts. Following the custom of those times at Lent, Haydn and Mozart collaborated in an oratorio called *The Obligation of the First Commandment,* Haydn composing the first part and Wolfgang the second. It was performed in March 1767 and its successful reception led to a further commission, an operetta, *Apollo et Hyacinthus,* which was performed at Salzburg University. Once more Leopold began to think of showing Wolfgang's talents to a wider audience and at that moment Vienna seemed just the

place; in the autumn the Archduchess Maria Josepha was to be married to King Ferdinand of Naples. In September 1767, therefore, Leopold and his son were once again in Vienna to seek their fortunes. However, before they had a chance to be heard at Court, an epidemic of smallpox broke out in the town and among its victims was the young Archduchess herself. All joy and celebrations ceased abruptly and the Mozarts left quickly, stopping at Olmitz near Vienna. But they were too late: Wolfgang had caught the disease and lay ill for weeks, even losing his sight for nine days. On returning to Vienna they found that a certain hostility had developed towards young Mozart amongst Viennese musicians, who were jealous of his popularity at court. The Emperor himself commissioned Mozart to write an opera, *La Finta semplice,* based on a comedy by Goldoni, but it was never performed in Vienna. Leopold believed that the jealous musicians headed by Gluck himself had schemed to prevent its presentation. Eventually it was performed in Salzburg in 1769.

Another view (left) of the Cathedral square, Salzburg. Apart from the festivals and entertainments of the pre-Christian era, the town was visited in medieval times by the best troubadours, summoned by the Archbishop. Paul Hothaimer, whom Paracelso called "the Dürer of music", was one of the chief glories of Salzburg.

Father Domenico Hagenauer (*above*), son of Johann Lorenz, was a faithful friend of Wolfgang Amadeus Mozart. He was born in 1744 and died in 1769. On the occasion of his ordainment to the priesthood in 1769, Mozart composed the so-called Domenicus Mass (*or* Mass in C Major, K 65). This sacred composition was first performed in the church of St. Peter, of which we see here on the left the rich baroque of the interior. Religion was a constant inspiration to him. Domenico Hagenauer's sister, Ursula, was a friend of Marianne.

33

Below, from the top: Innsbruck, Bolzano and Rovereto (Bertarelli Collection, Milan), the first 3 stops made by Mozart and his father on their journey to Italy in 1770. The two views to the right, from left to right, are Verona and Milan, where the 14-year-old Mozart had his first Italian successes.

Young Mozart's triumph at Verona was such that a rich admirer, Luigi Lugiati, commissioned a portrait of him, ascribed by some to Cignaroli but probably the work of Saverio della Rosa. It was then copied by the artist Bode in 1859 and reproduced in many prints, and is here shown on the left. (Mozarteum, Salzburg).

FIRST TRIP TO ITALY AND FIRST OPERA

The ever active Leopold now succeeded in obtaining permission from the Archbishop Sigismund to take his son to Italy, the great musical centre of the time. The art of many Austrian and German composers such as Gassman, Hasse, Christian and Emmanuel Bach, and Gluck, had been formed in the great Italian schools at Venice, Bologna, Naples and Rome, famous for their indisputable superiority. So Leopold and Wolfgang left for Italy on December 13, 1769; this time Nannerl stayed at home. Wolfgang was now nearly 14 years old. The two Mozarts reached Innsbruck on December 15 where Wolfgang gave a concert; a week later they were at Bolzano, and then Roveretto, where they were entertained by some old friends and pupils of Leopold's; at his first concert in Verona on January 17 the boy aroused indescribable enthusiasm: all the aristocratic families, amongst whom the most important were the Marquess Carlotti and Count Giusti del Giardino, talked of him. St. Thomas' church in Verona was always full for his organ recitals, and before he began to play two citizens would lift him shoulder high so that all could see the boy prodigy. Father and son reached Mantua on January 16, 1770 and Milan on the 23rd, where they found excellent lodgings with "heated beds" at the Augustine monastery of San Marco. The governor of Lombardy, Count Charles Joseph Firmian of Salzburg, introduced them to the Milanese salons and the festivities of the carnival. Mozart gave a private concert at the governor's own house and created such an impression that he was at once commissioned to write an opera to be presented in Milan at Christmas: this opera was to be *Mitridate Re di Ponto*. After a brief visit to Parma the Mozarts reached Bologna, their most important objective, on March 24, 1770; here reigned the famous Padre Martini. In one of Leopold's letters one reads: "Padre Martini spoke of Wolfgang with great amazement and tested him in many ways. After this my son's fame will travel throughout Italy because Padre Martini is the idol of the Italians". The future relationship between Wolfgang Amadeus Mozart and Padre Martini was not to be just one of the usual polite esteem, but a genuine bond of friendship and devotion. Despite the difference in their ages, their spirits were at one.

Top: portraits of Count Charles Joseph Firmian and Padre Giambaptista Martini. This precious spinet, shown above, is conserved in the Museum of Musical Instruments at the Sforzo Castle, Milan. The work of the famous harpsichord-maker, Antonio Scotti, it was made for Count Firmian in 1753 and was used by young Mozart during his first stay in Milan. On this elegant instrument, Mozart composed the opera Mitridate Re di Ponto, *first performed on the evening of December 25, 1770, at the Teatro Ducale, Milan. The keyboard is ebony inlaid with mother-of-pearl and is a typical example of 18th-century Milanese cabinet-making.*

At the time when the Mozarts were in Florence, Leopold I (below) was the Grand Duke of Tuscany, having succeeded his father in 1765. He brought substantial changes to Tuscany, draining the Val di Chiana swamps and introducing a modern penal code. On the death of his brother Joseph II in 1790, he became emperor.

AT HOME HE IS HONOURED BY THE POPE

Top right: the Tiber at Castel Sant'Angelo by Vanvitelli (Galleria d'Arte Antica e Moderno, Rome). Below, left: the cathedral square, Florence; right: the interior of the Sistine Chapel in the 18th century; In the centre: Clement XIV with a group of cardinals. Elected Pope in 1769, Giovanni Vincenzo Ganganelli suppressed the Jesuits in 1773. His name is linked with that of Pius VI by the Pio-Clementino Museum which he founded. Before being elected Pope, he had been an ardent preacher and a skilful teacher of theology and philosophy.

The Mozarts now directed themselves towards Florence, in the hope of finding the famous Italian spring weather: instead they met with rain, cold and violent winds which caused them both to catch colds as soon as they reached the city. Despite their indispositions, Leopold was so enthusiastic that he wrote to his wife in Salzburg: "Florence! I wish you could see it. One would like to live and die in such a place!" When they were both well again, they were received by the Grand Duke Leopold I, who deserves to be remembered for being the first European prince to abolish torture and the death penalty. Wolfgang played at Court together with the famous violinist, Pietro Nardini, and was greeted as usual by rapturous applause. Having arrived in Florence in the rain, the Mozarts left during a storm, and it took five days in a stagecoach on muddy, difficult roads to reach Rome, but as soon as they arrived they went to St. Peter's. In the Sistine Chapel there took place an incident which has become legendary. Wolgang was listening to the *Miserere* by Gregorio Allegri, of which it was forbidden, on pain of excommunication, to make any copies. This rule did not take into account Mozart's extraordinary memory however: he remembered it note for note and then, when he returned home, wrote it all down without any mistake or uncertainty. On May 12 the Mozarts attended a reception at the Vatican and saw the Pope. They succeeded in making their way through the Swiss Guards to the cardinals' table by virtue of their fine clothes and the fact that they spoke German and were, therefore, mistaken for nobility. They reached a position next to Cardinal Pallavicini, who, being curious, asked Wolfgang: "Would you mind telling me, confidentially, who you are?" On hearing the reply he exclaimed: "You? Are you, then, really the famous boy of whom one hears so much talk?" When they took their leave, Wolfgang kissed the cardinal's hand and the cardinal raised his cap as a sign of regard. When they returned to Rome after a visit to Naples, Pope Clement XIV conferred on Mozart the Order of the Cross of the Golden Spur, an honour which Gluck received when he was 40. Mozart received it as a youth of 14. His title meant that he could be addressed as "Chevalier Mozart", but he very seldom used it.

Right: Naples in the 18th century (Oest. Nationalbibliothek, Vienna). Bottom of the page, from the left: a masked ball at the San Carlo Theatre, Naples (Bibliothèque Nationale, Paris), and an 18th-century print showing the same theatre during a performance of an opera, always a great social occasion.

PRINCEPS

CAETERIQUE

ACADEMICI

PHYLHARMONICI.

Omnibus, et singulis praesentes Literas lecturis, felicitatem.

 Uamvis ipfa Virtus fibi, fuifque Sectatoribus gloriofum comparet Nomen, attamen pro majori ejufdem majeftate publicam in notitiam decuit propagari. Hinc eft, quòd hujufce noftrae PHYLHARMONICAE ACADEMIAE exiftimationi, & incremento confulere, fingulorumque Academicorum Scientiam, & profectum patefacere intendentes, Teftamur *Dominu Wolfgangu Amadeu Mozart e Salisburgo* fub die 9 Menfis *Octobris* Anni *1770* inter Academiae noftrae *Magiftros Compoftores* adfcriptum fuiffe. Tanti igitur Coacademici virtutem, & merita perenni benevolentiae monumento profequentes, hafce Patentes, Literas fubfcriptas, noftrique Confeffus Sigillo impreffo obfignatas dedimus.

Bononiae ex noftra Refidentia die *10* Menfis, *Octobris* Anni *1770*

Princeps. *Petronius Lanzi*

Mossius Xac Ferri Not.
a Secretis.

Regiftr. in Libro Camplono G *— pag. 147.*

Camplonerius

Above: the diploma of the Accademia Filarmonica of Bologna which Mozart received on becoming a member. He was unanimously elected by the jury on October 10, 1770. The examination for admission consisted of setting a Gregorian Antiphon for four voices in the contrapuntal style, taking due account of harmony and rhythm, which Wolfgang did with ease.

FROM NAPLES TO THE NORTH, STOPPING IN MILAN

At Naples their reception was overwhelming: even people in the streets waved and greeted him. Wolfgang was dressed in a suit of pink moiré lined with sky-blue silk and trimmed with silver lace. He wrote to his sister: "Vesuvius is giving off a lot of smoke today. We get up at 9 and often at 10, then we go out and eat at a *trattoria.* After lunch we write and then perhaps go out again." They were affably received by Queen Caroline and also visited the house of the English ambassador, William Hamilton. In the theatre, they heard operas by Piccini and Paisiello. They returned to Rome at the end of June, making the journey in only 27 hours. On arriving, Wolfgang was so exhausted that he fell asleep straight away and his father had to carry him to bed like a baby. Returning to Bologna, Wolfgang wrote a *Miserere* which so delighted Padre Martini that he proposed that the boy should become a member of the Accademia Filarmonica. The proposal was accepted even though the qualifying age for membership was 20. They hastened on to Milan to attend the premier of *Mitredate Re di Ponto,* which had been composed during this Italian trip. It was a triumphant success and the Milanese public called out "Evviva il maestrino!" With 130 *gigliati* in their purse and a commission for a new opera for the autumn, father and son visited Venice (which amazed them) and Padua, where Mozart played the organ in Santa Giustina. After a brief return to Salzburg which Wolfgang passed studying with his father and working on the commissions he had received in Italy, they returned again to Milan in August 1771 for the production of *Ascanio in Alba* to a libretto by Parini. The Archduke Ferdinand was to be married to Princess Beatrice of Modena on October 15 and *Ascanio in Alba* was presented the next day in honour of the occasion. It was a great success and was repeated several times; after hearing the opera, the famous composer Hasse is said to have remarked: "This boy will consign us all to oblivion." After their success, the Mozarts lingered in Milan until December 1771. They hoped that Mozart would be offered some musical post at court but none was forthcoming. On their return to Salzburg sad news awaited them: the archbishop was dead.

Top left: Giuseppe Parini and (right) another famous librettist, perhaps the most prolific of his time, Pietro Trapassi, better known as Metastasio. He wrote among other things the libretto for Betulia liberata *which Mozart set to music in 1771 and for* La Clemenza di Tito. *This tragedy with slight alterations by Mazola, the poet to the Court of Saxony,* served as the libretto for the opera which Mozart wrote in 1791. Centre: a picture of Queen Caroline of Naples, and the minutes of the meeting for Mozart's examination of admittance to the Accademia Filarmonica of Bologna. Above: St Steven's Square, Venice. Mozart's stay in Venice in 1771 was a particularly happy one.

While he was writing Ascanio *and* Lucio Silla, *Mozart also wrote a lot of religious music. "I have God constantly before my eyes. I realise his omnipotence and tremble before his wrath, but I recognize also his great love," he wrote. Opposite page: an imaginary portrait of Mozart seated at a harpsichord wearing a* rich dressing gown, by J. Duplessis, in the Louvre, Paris. Below: Heironymous Joseph Count of Colloredo, by Franz Xavier König (Mozarteum, Salzburg). Right: the title page of Lucio Silla. Bottom: Salzburg in spring. Apart from two short visits to Munich and Vienna, Mozart was in Salzburg from March 1773 to September 1777.*

"LUCIO SILLA": A SUCCESS BUT NOT A TRIUMPH

LUCIO SILLA
DRAMMA PER MUSICA
DA RAPPRESENTARSI
NEL REGIO-DUCAL TEATRO
DI MILANO
Nel Carnovale dell' anno 1773.
DEDICATO
ALLE LL. AA. RR.
IL SERENISSIMO ARCIDUCA
FERDINANDO
Principe Reale d' Ungheria , e Boemia , Arciduca d'Auftria, Duca di Borgogna , e di Lorena ec. , Cefareo Reale Luogo-Tenente , Governatore , e Capitano Generale nella Lombardia Auftriaca ,
E LA
SERENISSIMA ARCIDUCHESSA
MARIA RICCIARDA
BEATRICE D'ESTE
PRINCIPESSA DI MODENA.

IN MILANO,

Preffo Gio. Batifta Bianchi Regio Stampatore
Con licenza de' Superiori .

Archbishop Sigismund was greatly mourned, not only by Mozart whom his kindness had helped so much but by the whole of Salzburg. His successor, Heironymous Joseph Francis de Paula, Count Colloredo, was elected after much deliberation on March 14, 1772. If Sigismund had been modest, tolerant and generous, Colloredo was to be the opposite: arrogant, stern and austere. The occasion produced one satisfaction for Mozart however, perhaps the only one he was to have from Colloredo: the commission to write an opera, *Il sogno do Scipio*—to a text by Metastasio—for the celebrations to mark the accession of the new archbishop. He was also appointed concert master with a modest salary of 150 florins a year. In October, 1772, father and son returned to Italy to attend the production of the new opera *Lucio Silla,* which was presented at Milan on December 26. Although the opera received 26 performances it was not quite the triumph of previous occasions. Already Mozart was beginning to leave behind conventional modes of expression; his imagination was leading him to music which sounded strange to the ears of the average listener of the time. Once more the Mozarts delayed their return to Salzburg, making excuses to Colloredo; Leopold was trying to obtain a post for his son in Florence, but was unsuccessful. By March 1773 they had returned to Salzburg in time for the solemn entry of the archbishop. When at the beginning of the summer Colleredo left the town for his mountain retreat, leaving his staff free, Leopold and Wolfgang at once seized the opportunity to take themselves to Vienna where the Empress received them graciously. But Wolfgang's days as a child prodigy were over and interest in him had waned now that he had grown up. If Leopold had hoped to secure a post at court for his son, it was in vain. But although their summer in Vienna in 1773 produced little material gain, it did give Wolfgang the opportunity of hearing much good music, and meeting some of the greatest artists, amongst whom was Joseph Haydn, who remained his friend and teacher all his life: in the autumn, father and son returned to Salzburg. It was the end of September 1773, and there now began for Wolfgang a time of struggle as he tried to find the right post for his exceptional talents.

JOSEPH II COMES TO POWER

By the time Mozart returned to Vienna in the summer of 1773, the responsibility for government had passed from Maria Theresa to Joseph II, who did not have his mother's ability. He had the best intentions regarding reforms for the good of his people but these good intentions had poor results. Amongst other things, Joseph II ordered the closure of 700 monasteries in one year and tried to enforce the German language throughout his empire, without taking into account local customs and linguistic varieties. During Joseph II's reign there were in fact attempts at rebellion in Hungary and Belgium, and the application of many of these reforms had to be suspended. After the death of her husband, Francis of Loraine, Maria Theresa led a very retired life, losing interest in music and not going to theatres any more. Mozart was still received graciously at Court but in fact Maria Theresa no longer felt so well-disposed towards him. At this time the harpsichord was gradually being superseded by the pianoforte, invented by Bartolomeo Cristofori. During his childhood Mozart still used the harpsichord with plucked strings, but things were changing quickly and confronted by the new instrument musicians found themselves obliged to learn new techniques and even new music. In Bartolomeo's invention, the strings of the instrument were struck by hammers worked by a simple system of springs linked to the keys, instead of being plucked by quills. The sound could be modified to various shades of loud and soft, depending on the pressure applied by the finger. For many years the tone was still very thin but after Cristofori's time the pedal was invented which lifted the cloth dampers from the strings, so that the sound could be prolonged as desired. It was only in the 19th century, by the time of Beethoven and Chopin, that the sonority of the pianoforte was improved by replacing the wooden supporting frame with one of iron, making it able to support greater strain and larger strings. Thus when one speaks of Mozart's piano, one must think of an instrument with a very much softer sound, and less variation in the piano and forte. He had played an early piano while in Italy in 1770 but it was very different from the pianos of today.

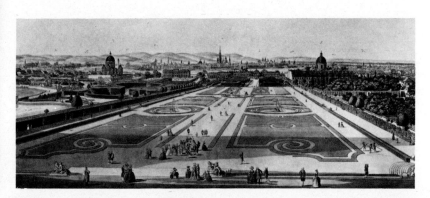

Top: between the picture of the market-place in Vienna and a view of the Belvedere Palace (Oest Bibliothek, Vienna), are portraits of Sylvester and Sigmund von Barisani (Mozarteum, Salzburg). The Barisani brothers were among Mozart's childhood friends. One of their sisters was also one of his youthful loves. Later when they moved to Vienna, Sigmund Barisani was Mozart's doctor. Above, across 2 pages: a coloured print of the Kohlmarkt, Vienna, where Mozart lived in the spring of 1783. Like Beethoven, Mozart also had many different homes, often being obliged to move for financial reasons, although not so much as Beethoven. From the autumn of 1781 until his marriage he lived at no. 3 in the Graben, and returned to no. 591 in the same street from January to September 1784. Left: Mozart at the court of Joseph II. Mozart had hoped for much from the Emperor but was to be disappointed. In 1768, he wrote La Finta Semplice at the suggestion of Joseph II, but Joseph omitted to provide the necessary money for the production, while Leopold was convinced that the impresario who ran the opera house was an enemy.

Far right: Munich at the time when the Mozarts went there for the production of La Finta Giardiniera, *which was commissioned by the Elector of Bavaria, Maximillian III (right). The Elector, however, did not want to take Mozart into his service and his later efforts to this purpose were in vain, despite the good* offices and recommendations of *his friend and patron, the Bishop of Chiemsee, Count Zeill (below left). Below, right: Mozart in 1773 (an unsigned miniature on ivory). According to Robert Bory, an expert on Mozart portraiture, it was probably painted in Milan and taken home by Wolfgang as a present for his sister.*

A NEW OPERA IS PRODUCED AT MUNICH

The dull days at Count Colloredo's court were suddenly brightened by good news: the prince-bishop of Chiemsee had obtained for Mozart the commission to write an *opera buffa* for the Munich Carnival of 1775. The Prince-Pallatine of Munich, Maximilian III, a cultured and musical man who himself played the viola da gamba excellently, greatly admired Mozart. Not wishing to quarrel with the powerful Elector of Bavaria, Colloredo grudgingly gave the Mozarts permission to go to Munich. They arrived on December 6, 1774 in freezing weather and Wolfgang suffered an attack of bronchitis, but he soon recovered and was able to attend to the preparation of the new opera, *La Finta Giardiniera,* on a libretto by Ranieri de Calzabigi. Many people from Salzburg travelled to Munich for the new opera, including Mozart's sister. Mozart himself refers to the success of the opera in a letter to his mother, who had stayed at home: "Praise be to God, *La Finta Giardiniera* was put on yesterday, the 13th, and turned out so well that I cannot possibly describe to you the furore. The theatre was so jammed full that many people had to be turned away. After every aria there was a regular thunder of clapping and shouts of *'viva Maestro'!"* Colloredo also went to Munich but he waited until after the *première* and did not attend any of the performances. When someone started singing young Mozart's praises to him he could only respond by bowing his head and shrugging his shoulders. Mozart stayed in Munich to enjoy the carnival, which was in full swing, and to compose a variety of incidental music. At this time Mozart also wrote a motet and sent a copy to Padre Martini for his criticism. His comment was: "It is with pleasure that I have studied this motet from beginning to end and I say with all sincerity that I am singularly pleased to find in it all that is required of modern music: good harmony, mature modulation, a moderate pace in the violins . . ." Mozart returned to Salzburg on March 7, 1775. Here he composed his first piano concerto (*K 175*), the *Symphony in G Minor* (*K 183*), the *violin concerto in A* (*K 219*) and the *Divertimenti K 251* and 252. If his childhood compositions had shown the influence of J. C. Bach, Hasse, Samartini, Tartini or Bocherini, the most important influence on him now was that of Joseph Haydn.

Right: a side view of Salzburg Cathedral at midday. Many of Mozart's religious works were heard for the first time in this cathedral. (Bibliothèque Nationale, Paris). Below: the Palace of the Counts of Lodron to whom Mozart dedicated one of his concertos (Municipal Museum, Salzburg).

LEAVING FOR ANOTHER GREAT JOURNEY

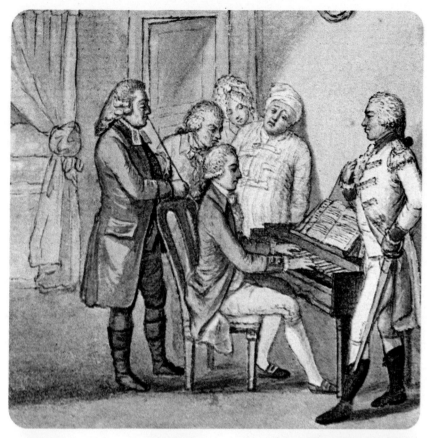

Wolfgang loved his father very deeply, indeed one could even say he worshipped him. It was only his subservient attitude towards Colloredo which annoyed him: with the years such subservience had become insupportable to Wolfgang. One wonders what might have become of Mozart if his father had left him more to himself and been less strict about his education, if he had not always been near to guide him, defend him and encourage him. His music might well have been more experimental. At 18, Wolfgang was still immature as an adult: sensitive and gay, a dreamer who had no practical sense. In Italy, England and his own Austria he had become accustomed to success, praise and adulation, while the austere Colloredo denied him the slightest request. Wolfgang had become very popular with the gay Salzburg aristocracy who had come to consider him as a musical "gentleman servant". All the noble drawing rooms without exception resounded every evening with the delightful music which flowed from the inexhaustible imagination of the young artist. In 1777 alone he wrote the *Missa Brevis* K 275, the *quartet K 285*, the *violin concerto in D, K 271* and the *piano concerto in E flat, K 271*. Every day the creative impulse in him became more urgent: the beautiful aristocratic ladies would gaze interestedly at him when his face was lit up with inspiration. But there was growing in him a sense of oppression at his servile position, which he felt was unfitting for a great artist. Salzburg had become too confined for him: he decided to seek his fortunes in Munich. Leopold wanted to accompany him as he had always done in the past but Colloredo refused him leave, threatening to dismiss him. The Mozarts could not afford to lose this income and therefore Wolfgang set off for Munich with his mother. Leopold had to borrow money to make sure that Wolfgang wanted for nothing. Furnished with various letters of recommendation, Wolfgang and his mother left Salzburg at dawn on September 23, 1777. Leopold was busy giving advice and recommendations, running from room to room seeing that nothing was forgotten right up to the last minute: finally, as the horses galloped off, nothing remained but for him to bless his wife and son from the window.

Top: Mozart in Salzburg playing for a group of friends (Municipal Museum, Salzburg). It was not that Mozart lacked admirers or friends at Salzburg, for he was the most outgoing and loving character, but that he felt cut off in the little town at the foot of the mountains. Mozart was above all continually seeking a permanent position at the court of some prince. Many were the efforts he *made to this end, but all in vain. Once, much later on, he even applied to the King of Prussia. Certainly, his dislike of Salzburg became ever more intense as years went by: "Here there is little fortune to be made with music." Above, left: an old street in the town and right: Mozart's harpsichord in a room of the house where he was born, now transformed into a museum.*

HE FALLS IN LOVE WITH ALOYSIA

Mozart reached Munich in 1777, his 21st year. He at once contacted the old friends who had previously helped and encouraged him, Count Joseph Anton von Seau and the Bishop of Chiemsee, Count Ferdinand Christoph von Zeill. After playing in the great houses of the nobility, always to great applause and admiration, he offered his services to the Elector of Bavaria who, however, politely declined them as he was afraid of incurring the bad will of Colloredo. Mozart remained cheerful, but his patient mother was lonely when her son had to leave her alone in their lodgings. Although far away his father followed all their activities and persuaded his son to quit Munich for Augsburg, his own birthplace, where he wanted Wolfgang to become known to his fellow citizens. He showered his wife and son with letters of advice. In Augsburg, mother and son stayed at the house of an uncle, Franz Mozart. It was here that Mozart met and fell in love with his cousin, Maria Tecla, but it was a lighthearted and rather superficial relationship and did not leave much trace on their hearts. From Augsburg, Wolfgang moved on to Mannheim, a city famous for its culture. Here the Prince Palatine took an intense personal interest in music, patronising artists who came there. It was a visit of great importance for Wolfgang: his genius was immediately appreciated at Mannheim. He gave lessons and concerts, attended theatres and passed many evenings in society drawing-rooms. But the hope of finding some more permanent post seemed just as remote here as elsewhere. The *Symphony in D major, K 297,* the *Sonata for piano and violin, K 296* and the *Piano Sonatas K 330* and *331* all date from this period. During his stay in Mannheim Wolfgang gave some music to be copied to Fridolin Weber, a singer and distant relation of Carlo Maria von Weber. They got on very well together, became good friends and soon Mozart got to know the whole family: Frau Weber and her four daughters, Josepha, Aloysia, Constanze and Sofia. Wolfgang at once fell in love with Aloysia. It was his first real love after many youthful infatuations. On January 17, 1778, he wrote telling his father that he had met a girl who had the most beautiful, pure voice. This letter resulted in an order from Leopold to leave Mannheim for Paris.

V. AMADEO WOLFGANGO MOZART ACCAD·FILARMON:DI BOLOG
DI VERONA

This portrait of Mozart (left) was said by those who knew him to be an 'absolute likeness'. The original, whose author is unknown, was lost, but this copy which hangs in the Liceo Musicale, Bologna, is dated 1777. Dedicated to Padre Martini, it shows Mozart wearing the golden cross of the Papal Order.

Above: Mozart's famous little cousin, Anna Maria Tecla, whom he met in Augsburg in 1777. This portrait, which she gave her cousin as a present, is dated 1778 when she was 20. Certainly the letters Mozart wrote to Anna Maria are amongst his gayest and most relaxed. It was, however, a romance without a sequel. Papa Mozart saw to it that things were not allowed to take too serious a turn. Left: the market square at Mannheim. The Elector, Prince Carlo Teodoro, was a great patron of the German theatre. On the facing page: the elegant rococo drawing-room at Nymphenburg Castle.

49

Below: the Palace of the Tuileries, a painting by F. Raguenet (Carnavalet Museum, Paris). It was in the Swiss room of this palace that the "concerts spirituels" were held. It was at one of these evenings that Mozart's Symphony in D, composed in 1778, was performed for the first time. From left to right: some of the people whose names are linked with Mozart's stay in Paris: Nicola Piccinni, P. La Houssaye, François Joseph Gossec, Joseph le Gros and the Baron Grimm. Two operas and an opera buffa by Piccinni were performed at Paris theatres while Mozart was staying there.

HIS MOTHER DIES: MOZART RETURNS SADLY TO PARIS

With his heart in turmoil at having to leave Mannheim and Aloysia Weber, Mozart, together with his mother, finally reached Paris at the end of March, 1778, after $9\frac{1}{2}$ days in the stage coach. They found lodgings in the Rue du Gros Chenet. Paris, a city of some half a million inhabitants, was the intellectual centre of Europe. Louis XVI had recently ascended the throne but the way to revolution was already in preparation. At first Mozart did not quite know what to do. His father wrote urging him to go into society and visit all the people who might be able to help him. He called upon his old friend Baron von Grimm but did not find him as affable as before. However he struck up a good relationship with Joseph Le Gros, the director of the "concerts spirituels", and it was at one of these concerts that his *Symphony in D, K 297,* later called the *Paris Symphony,* was performed for the first time. It was soon after this concert that Mozart's mother fell ill with a fever. They called a doctor who prescribed rhubarb dipped in wine. When informed of her indisposition, Baron Grimm visited her and sent his own doctor. But she grew worse and finally, after receiving the last sacrament, died on Friday, July 3, 1778. Wolfgang wrote: "I have never seen anyone die, and thus it has befallen that the first death I should see was that of my own mother." Baron Grimm lent Wolfgang 15 *louis d'or* for the funeral expenses of his mother. Mozart had tried to prepare his father for the sad news by writing to say that his mother was very ill when she was in fact already dead. He asked a friend to break the news to him. Leopold now wanted Wolfgang to return to Salzburg, promising that things would be different in future and his position as court composer assured. Grimm wrote to Leopold expressing the opinion that Wolfgang was not really robust enough to cope with the conditions prevailing in Paris at that time; that he was "too kind hearted, too easily deceived . . . I wish he had, for the sake of his success, half as much talent and twice as much shrewdness". Finally Wolfgang was reluctantly persuaded to return to Salzburg. He left Paris on September 26, 1778, taking with him various compositions which he had worked on during his six months in Paris: among them the *sonata for violin and piano, K 296,* and the *piano sonatas K 330 and 331.*

PUBLIC APPLAUSE AND CRITICAL INDIFFERENCE FOR "IDOMINEO"

Below: Salzburg today. After the unhappy outcome of Wolfgang's journey, Leopold Mozart did all he could to persuade his son to return home. Leopold, who like his son, became a freemason, loved his son deeply and showed great zeal as a teacher, guided always by a faith in the ideals of the era of enlightenment.

Wolfgang made several short visits on his way home to Salzburg: he stopped at Nancy, Strasburg and Mannheim, and he spent his birthday in Munich where he found Aloysia Weber, by now an admired and established singer. But she did not return his affections and was already engaged to an actor, Joseph Lange. His passionate avowal of love being rejected, he sat down at the piano and sang "gladly I leave the girl who does not want me", but in fact he suffered intensely from this refusal. His cousin, Anna Maria Tecla, who had come to Munich at the beginning of January in response to his request, did her best to comfort him and together they returned to Salzburg in January 1779, where they were greeted once more by Leopold and Nannerl. Thus Wolfgang returned home to live with his sister, the dogs and the birds: the archbishop offered him the post of organist at 450 gulden a year, promising to allow him one voyage every two years and to prepare his works for performance abroad. Colloredo also commissioned Mozart to compose a mass (the so-called *Coronation Mass*), anthems, vespers and organ sonatas; besides these he also wrote, either for private commissions or from inspiration, two symphonies, a symphonia concertante, two serenades, a concerto for two pianos, a piano sonata and a sonata for violin. Day by day Leopold could hear his son's new music at home, but he was not always pleased, sometimes finding it too complex both in style and inspiration. While he had been away, Wolfgang had begun to develop in quite a different way from that which Leopold had intended. When Wolfgang had gone to Munich to complete *Idomineo*, commissioned by the Prince of Bavaria, Leopold had advised him to use a "popular style". And Wolfgang replied: "Don't give it a thought: in my work there is music for every type of person except those with asses ears". The Empress Maria Theresa died on November 29, 1780, but after a brief period of mourning the theatres opened again and *Idomineo* was presented on January 29th, two days after Mozart's twenty-fifth birthday. The Elector attended, as did large numbers of the public, and in spite of certain critics it was a considerable success.

Left: a painting of the Madonna in the Shrine of St. Mary, and the shrine itself near Salzburg. Mozart was inspired by this painting to compose the Coronation Mass. When writing home after his mother's death, he asked that, if they had not already done so, a memorial service be celebrated for her at St. Mary's.

Below: the Mozart family painted by Giovanni Nepomuceno della Croce, with a portrait of their mother hanging on the wall. (Mozarteum, Salzburg). The painting was done in 1789, eleven years after her death. Wolfgang Amadeus and his sister Marianna are seated at the piano: on the right is Leopold, holding a violin.

53

THE FINAL BREAK WITH HIS PATRON

Facing page: the Teutonic Knights' House in Vienna where Mozart stayed at the beginning of 1781, together with the prince-archbishop's other servants, while he was still in his employ. Below, right is the portrait of Colloredo from a print in the Bibliothèque Nationale, Paris. On the left is Muzio Clementi, whose studies *have wearied so many young people learning to play the piano. On December 24, 1781, there took place between him and Mozart a sort of musical contest in the presence of the Emperor Joseph II. He decided, after hearing them play, that Clementi played "with artistry" while Mozart interpreted "with artistry and taste".*

While Wolfgang was enjoying the pleasures of the carnival at Munich, the compelling voice of the Archbishop Colloredo recalled him: he was to repair at once to Vienna where the archbishop had gone to pay homage to the Emperor Joseph II, who had succeeded his mother. Colloredo had perhaps begun to realise Mozart's musical merits and jealously desired that he should not undertake any activities outside the court. In Vienna, Colloredo lived in a large three-storied palace near the cathedral of St. Steven and he wished Mozart to attend him there. Mozart obeyed, but he soon realised that as "archbishop's musician" he was just another of the archbishop's "private servants" which meant he was obliged to present himself every day at certain times, and often wait on the Archbishop at the homes of other nobles like a common servant. At lunch he had for company, two valets, the auditor, the confectioner and two cooks. Writing to his father, Wolfgang describes the scene: "Please note that the two valets sit at the head of the table. But at least I have the honour of being seated above the cooks". After the success of *Idomineo*, Mozart felt even more profoundly the humiliation of his treatment in Vienna. Colloredo even refused him permission to take part in a benefit concert for musicians' orphans, even though he was not going to play any of his own works, and although the Archbishop later yielded it was yet another humiliation for Mozart. Thus, a strong sense of rebellion was born in him and he wrote to his father that: "it does not please our beloved archbishop that his servants earn money, only that they lose it". When Colloredo ordered Mozart to return to Salzburg, he disobeyed. A stormy scene followed between the archbishop and the excited musician, during which Colloredo lost control and hurled abuse at Mozart, calling him a rascal and a villain. Mozart at once presented his resignation to the archbishop's major-domo, Count Arco. With him also there were harsh words and it ended with the count expelling him. Mozart had been treated like the most menial of servants, but he had had the courage to revolt and at last he was free. He was the first musician to rebel against the establishment, and reaffirmed the dignity of the artist for future generations.

Above: Aloysia Weber, one of the four daughters of Fridolin and Maria Cecilia (née Stamm), as Zelinda in Grétry's opera Azor and Zelinda. *Right: Aloysia in later life. In 1780 she had married the actor Joseph Lange. Aloysia was born in 1760 and died in 1830. Wolfgang fell in love with her at first sight—she was then only 17.*

Mozart had many plans for her and wanted to go to Italy with Weber: he was convinced not only of her love but of her artistic talent. But Aloysia, who at first had given him hope, showed indifference but a few months later. Mozart was bitterly disillusioned, but it is obvious that she was not really worthy of him.

Leopold's consent to the marriage arrived too late. He was never satisfied with his daughter-in-law, and, it would seem, not without reason. Some say this marriage was a gross error in Mozart's life. Constanze would annoy her husband by violent scenes of jealousy and she only really began to understand and appreciate him when she lost him. In 1809 she married the Danish Councillor of State, George Nicholas von Niseen. In 1828 they published a biography of Mozart which, based on the original documents, is still one of the most important documents for Mozartian study. Below, left: St. Steven's Church, Vienna, where Mozart and Constanze were married; right, the couple in 1783: two prints taken from miniatures, the originals of which have been lost; the marriage contract dated August 4, 1782. Facing page: a portrait of Constanze Mozart in 1802 by Hans Hansen. Constanze had already been a widow for 11 years. (Mozarteum, Salzburg).

WEDDING TO CONSTANZE OPPOSED

After breaking with Colloredo, Mozart left his rooms in the archbishop's palace and took lodgings at the house of his friends the Webers. Fridolin Weber had died and his wife, Maria Cecilia Stamm, took lodgers, aided by her three unmarried daughters, Josepha, Sofia and Constanze. The fourth had married the German actor Joseph Lange and was making her career in the opera houses of Europe. Thus the Webers, mother and daughters, cared for Wolfgang and gave him moral support at the time of his dramatic crisis with the archbishop. Above all, the modest and gentle Constanze showed him much tenderness and Wolfgang was at once attracted to her. Though not wildly in love he wanted to settle down. When Leopold heard of Wolfgang's second attachment to one of the Weber girls, he ordered his son to change his lodgings. By this time Wolfgang's heart was quite conquered, nevertheless he obeyed and moved house but only to protect his beloved from gossip. The ingenuous and honest Mozart was at one time threatened with an ultimatum by Herr Thorwarth, guardian to the Weber girls: either cease visiting or sign an undertaking to marry Constanze within three years with a penalty of 300 florins a year if he broke his promise. Wolfgang duly signed but when the guardian had gone, Constanze tore up the paper saying: "I need no written assurances from you, dear Mozart, I believe in your word and it is enough for me". Sometimes the lovers' happiness was clouded by little misunderstandings: Constanze once confessed to Wolfgang that she had let a young cavalier measure the calves of her legs! But they were soon reconciled again. Mozart's new opera, *Die Entführung aus dem Serail*, was produced at this time with great success, but despite this Leopold did not consent to the wedding. Then Constanze quarelled with her mother, ran away from home and took refuge with one Baroness von Waldstädten. At this Wolfgang decided to marry her whatever the cost, and on a hot August day in 1782 they were married. Wolfgang was 27 and Constanze 18. A week later, he wrote to his father: "When we 2 were married, my wife and I, we began to cry: and at once everyone else began to cry too . . ." It was the year of the *Haffner Symphony* and the *Piano Concerto K 415*.

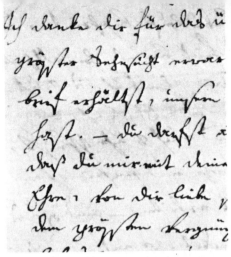

Below: Marianne Mozart and her husband about 1785 by an unknown artist (Mozarteum, Salzburg). On August 23, 1784, Marianne Mozart married Baron Johann Baptist Berchthold von Sonnenburg (1736–1801), a widower with five children, and a councillor at the Court of Salzburg. He was 15 years older than his wife who outlived him by many years: Marianne died in 1829. Right: a fragment of a letter from Mozart to his sister dated February 13, 1782, thanking her for sending the libretto of Idomineo and describing his busy days in Vienna. Like all the letters he wrote to his sister, its shows his great affection for her.

NANNERL TOO FINDS A HUSBAND

Mozart found great happiness and contentment in his marriage, in the peace of their home and their mutual love. Constanze rather lacked sense and made little administrative errors, but Wolfgang was content and did not ask of her more than she could give. Constanze also had a lovely voice, played the piano, had musical taste and left her husband in peace while he was composing. No event, whether happy or sad, ever cut across his artistic work. A child, Raimund Leopold, was born in June 1783. In the same year, father and son were formally reconciled. Wolfgang and Constanze, therefore, visited Salzburg though they were coldly received by Leopold and Nannerl who were yet to be reconciled to the marriage. Even when the *Mass in C minor,* which Wolfgang had brought with him, was performed with Constanze singing and Wolfgang conducting, they did not unbend. On their way back to Vienna, the Mozarts stopped at Linz where Wolfgang hurriedly wrote a symphony, which later came to be called the *Linz Symphony,* one of his most inspired and beautiful works. Great was their distress however, when they arrived home, to find that their "fat little baby" had died suddenly and was already in his grave. Such deaths were much more expected however, in the 18th century. Leopold Mozart decided to go to Vienna to return the visit. Nannerl stayed at Salzburg because by now she, too, was married, to the magistrate Johann Baptist von Sonnenburge, a widower with five children. It was a marriage of convenience, but the placid Nannerl coped very well. Leopold often wrote to his daughter from Vienna, telling her how he had met Joseph Haydn, and that he had attended a concert of Wolfgang's music: in these letters it seems that for a while his former fatherly pride was reborn. It was the year of the *Quartet K 458, Sonata K 457* for the piano, and the *Concertos K 451* and *459.* The couple had moved house and now had at their disposal a large bedroom, a spacious dining room and two drawing rooms for dancing or entertaining. Leopold was satisfied with this menage and at peace with his pleasant daughter-in-law. Before long another baby, Charles, was born. By the middle of April 1785 Leopold Mozart had to return to his beloved Salzburg. It had been their last meeting.

Mozart was 24 years younger than Haydn and greatly admired him: he called him "the father of the symphony and the quartet". (We see them together in the engraving at the bottom of the page.) Their friendship began during one of Haydn's short visits to Vienna. Mozart dedicated six beautiful quartets to him, written between 1783–5. Below: a masonic lodge in the 18th century. Mozart, devoutly religious and a regular church-goer, joined the freemasons, as has been noted, who advocated the advancement of liberal thought. Right: St. Peter's church, near which lived the widow Weber, who sheltered Mozart after his break with Colloredo.

HAYDN IS HIS FRIEND, THE INTRIGUERS ARE HIS ENEMIES

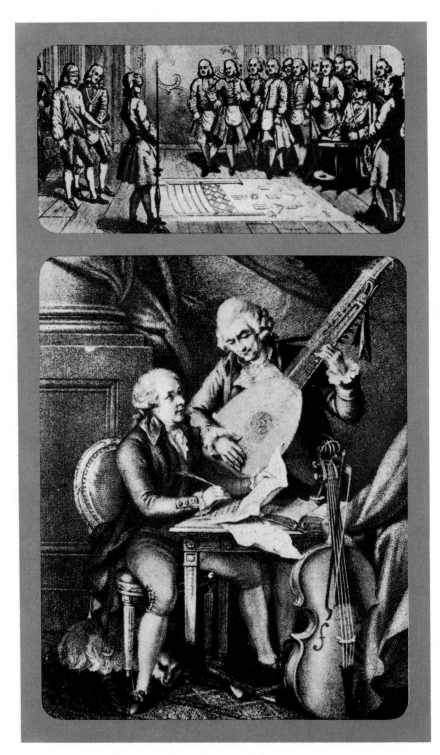

The years in Vienna from 1783 to 1786 were important ones in Mozart's development. Baron Gottfried van Swieten who had been Austrian ambassador to Berlin returned to Vienna to become director of the court library; he loved above all the music of Handel and Bach and organized musical evenings to which Mozart was always invited. Mozart too, revered Handel and Bach above all. At that time Bach was known only to a select few and it was not until the 19th century that Mendelssohn was to rediscover him. Mozart was familiar with all styles and with an enormous amount of old music but it was the perfect contrapuntal art of Bach which moved and excited him most: for him this was the essence of pure music and such was his enthusiasm that he transcribed five Bach fugues for stringed instruments. During this period in Vienna the friendship between Mozart and Haydn deepened. "I, as an honest man, tell you before God that your son is the greatest composer of our times. He has taste and, moreover, a thorough knowledge of composition", wrote Haydn to Leopold Mozart. Between 1783 and 1786 Mozart wrote the *Piano Sonata K 457,* the *Piano Concerto K 459* and the *Prague Symphony.* The Vienna of these years was a rich and lively city: the population had increased and devoted its wealth to the arts and sciences: it was a centre of culture, thought and progress. In spite of the censor a spirit of generous tolerance prevailed. Even freemasonry was tolerated and was widely practised by some of the greatest intellectuals of the time. Mozart and his father were both freemasons, though Catholics. This was Mozart's happiest period: he had a happy home and a sweet affectionate little wife, and his career seemed to be progressing from one triumph to another. When the weather was fine the couple would go to the Prater of an afternoon, dine there and linger till the dusk of the evening. But every new success, especially in the theatre, made enemies for Mozart, who banded together against him. To fight this hidden hostility was too much for this man who was quite without cunning. One of his most relentless enemies was Antonio Salieri, and the ingenuous Mozart fell easily into the traps laid for him and became enmeshed in difficulties from which he was unable to extricate himself.

Below: some of the people linked with Mozart's life in Vienna. They are (from the top): Antonio Salieri, Joseph Haydn, Hummel (who was his pupil) and Paisiello. Salieri, Joseph II's great favourite, was responsible for leading a sordid intrigue against Mozart as he was afraid of being replaced as Imperial Kapellmeister.

PRAGUE TRIUMPH OF "THE MARRIAGE OF FIGARO"

It was in Baron von Wetzlar's house that Mozart met Lorenzo da Ponte, a Venetian poet who had come to Vienna to work with Metastasio. He had started writing about Figaro, the character who had become notorious with Paisiello's *The Barber of Seville*, based on Beaumarchais' comedy, *Le Mariage de Figaro*. This had taken Paris by storm in 1784 and created quite a scandal because of the way the servant-master relationship was presented: Louis XVI had only allowed it to be played before a select private audience. Da Ponte prepared a libretto of *The Marriage of Figaro* intending it for either Mozart or Salieri. Having quarrelled with Salieri, he offered it to Mozart and thus began the collaboration which resulted in three more masterpieces. Mozart fell in love with both the subject and the character: he and Da Ponte took some months to complete the work. When it became known that Mozart was working on a new opera, his enemies attacked and denigrated his work. But Lorenzo da Ponte, already worried about the subject which had created such a furore in France, went himself to the emperor and assured him that Mozart's opera was going to be a masterpiece. Hardly had the emperor given his approval than Mozart's enemies tried to convince the singers that the opera was technically impossible and that they would all be made fools of. However, in spite of everything the opera was presented triumphantly on May 1, 1786, with so many encores being called that it went on nearly twice as long as expected. While calls of "long live the great Mozart" came from the auditorium, the orchestra showed their enthusiasm by rising to their feet and banging their instruments with their bows. The success was repeated every evening and earned for Mozart a 100 ducats; after that the opera was in the hands of the impresarios. Although Mozart's health was gradually declining (he suffered frequently from sickness and fevers and other disturbances) he continued to give lessons and to accept invitations to play—indeed he still had to live by them. While he enjoyed life in this pleasure-loving Vienna and frequently came home late at night, his financial position was becoming precarious. But now there arrived unexpectedly an invitation to go to Prague where he was to be triumphantly received.

Above, in colour: The National Hof Theatre, where The Marriage of Figaro *was produced in 1786. The opera, begun by Mozart in the autumn of 1785, was only finished in April 1786 after the composer had interrupted his work in January to write the operetta* The Impresario. *Top: two of Léon Camus's designs for the first Paris production of* The Marriage of Figaro *in the 19th century. (Bibliothèque de l'Opéra, Paris); below: next to the portrait of*

Beaumarchais, are those of two of the most famous interpreters of the opera: Barilli as the Countess and Schieroni as Susanna (Museo Teatrale alla Scala, Milan). Pierre-Augustin Caron de Beaumarchais wrote La Folle Journée ou le Mariage de Figaro *as a sequel to his successful comedy* Le Barbier de Séville. *Facing page: The inn in Griechenstrasse near the cathedral where Mozart often went with his friends and where they have a copy of his signature.*

THE MASTERPIECE
"DON GIOVANNI"

In Bohemia the effects of the wars of the 17th-century could still be seen but in Prague the arts, in particular music and French and Italian culture, were flourishing. Many families could afford the luxury of maintaining a private orchestra. The Duscheks, friends of Mozart, particularly liked to invite some of the best musicians to gatherings at their beautiful villa on the outskirts of the city. After the first performances in Vienna, Prague quickly welcomed *Die Entführung aus dem Serail* and *The Marriage of Figaro* to her theatres, and now Mozart was there to direct them himself. By now Mozart's music was tremendously popular and the composer was invited everywhere; one concert alone earned him 1,000 florins. The friendliness and enthusiasm of Prague stimulated in Wolfgang the desire to dedicate a new opera to his Bohemian friends. The Italian impresario, Bondini, seized upon the idea and at once engaged Mozart, paying him 100 ducats: the new opera was to be called *Don Giovanni* and was to be an unrivalled success. For nearly two centuries this play, taken from the 17th-century Spanish drama *El Burlador de Sevilla* by Tirso da Molina, had passed from theatre to theatre, undergoing many alterations

and modifications. To Mozart, however, the protagonist was not just a vulgar libertine but a renaissance character, an aristocrat, an exceptional man but without morals or scruples. Lorenzo da Ponte at once set himself to work on the libretto with a bottle of Tockay and some Spanish tobacco on the table and a young and pretty secretary to help and to amuse him. In this atmosphere, the libretto went along very well and Mozart was at once pleased with it. The opera was produced in Prague on October 29, 1787, an historic date for the history of music. It was received with overwhelming success and Wolfgang himself wrote to his librettist: "My opera had its first performance and was received with the greatest applause." On May 7, 1788, *Don Giovanni* was given in Vienna but the Prague success was not repeated. Joseph II commented: "Such music is not meat for the teeth of my Viennese", to which Mozart replied: "Give them time to chew on it". Wolfgang's father did not witness this new triumph of his son: he died at the age of 62 on May 28, 1787, with Nannerl at his side. Wolfgang only heard the news afterwards. Now for the first time he had to make his own choices and decisions, unaided.

Facing page, top: the title page
of the first edition of Don
Giovanni, published in 1801 in
Leipzig. Far left: a scene from
Squarzina's production of Don
Giovanni for the 1965–6 season at
La Scala, Milan (scenery by
R. Allio, costumes by
Guglielminetti). The portraits are
centre of page: Sontag; centre
right: Teresa Saporiti (who created
the part) and bottom right: Luisa
Gutsman Meyer—three famous
interpreters of Donna Anna.
Bottom left: Lorenzo da Ponte
(1740–1838), equally famous as an
adventurer and a poet. Although of
Jewish origin, he became a priest.
Above: Mozart playing some
extracts from his new opera before
a group of some Viennese admirers.
(Museo Teatrale alla Scala, Milan).
Left: the decree of December 7, 1787,
nominating Mozart "musician to
the Imperial Chapel," with an
annual income of 800 florins. His
reply to this proposition was: "It
is too much for what I do but too
little for what I could do." He
meant that instead of composing
music for court balls, he would have
preferred to have been entrusted
with the composition of more
important works, operas in
particular. Mozart's poverty
was aggravated by the
fact that there were no
copyright laws.

In April, 1789, the young Prince Charles Lichnowsky invited Mozart to accompany him to Berlin. They left Vienna on April 8, stopping first at Prague, a city particularly dear to Mozart. (Below: Prague in a coloured 18th-century print). Passing through Dresden and Leipzig, they finally arrived in Berlin on April 25.

However, Mozart's hopes of this journey were in vain and at the end of May he returned to Vienna. Bottom left: Frederick William II of Prussia and (right) an unfinished (although not the last) portrait of Mozart by Lange, painted about 1783. Centre: a poster giving details of a performance of Cosi fan tutte. Right: a street and

St. Thomas's Church, Leipzig. It was when Mozart played a Bach chorale on the famous organ of this church on April 20, 1789, that he aroused such enthusiasm in his listeners. Below right: Karl and Wolfgang Amadeus junior, born in 1784 and 1791. Karl was a gifted amateur and Wolfgang a professional musician.

AT LEIPZIG THEY SAID THE GREAT BACH HAD RETURNED

After his triumph in Prague, the miserable conditions of his life in Vienna seemed unbearable. To earn his living he had to compose for the Court, for the bourgeoisie, for the people: dances, waltzes, serenades, a little of everything, but all were jewels created by the intellect of genius. Mozart had a struggle to pay the rent and was obliged to move house at least six times. The only financial help came from a friend and fellow-mason, Michael Puchberg. It was in Vienna that Mozart is said to have met a seventeen-year-old youth called Ludwig van Beethoven. In 1789, Mozart once again hoped to improve his fortunes abroad. Together with his pupil, Prince Charles von Lichnowsky, who paid the expenses, he left for Berlin on April 8, with the idea of giving concerts and of finding some means which would enable him to leave Vienna for good. They visited Leipzig where Mozart played on the great organ used by Johann Sebastian Bach and Johann Frederick Doles, an old pupil of Bach's, on hearing such great playing, exclaimed: "I believed that perhaps my master had returned to the world!" In Berlin, Mozart was warmly welcomed. Frederick William II of Prussia loved the arts and he was himself a good cellist, but he was surrounded by musicians and all the available musical posts were occupied. Afraid of provoking rivalry, the king did not even invite Mozart to give a concert; he did, however, send a purse of 100 gold coins. This trip to Berlin, therefore, had not served any purpose. On May 28, Mozart returned to Vienna to find the creditors about to sequester his property and once again his friend Puchberg came to his aid. Constanze had been ill; they owed large sums to the doctors and now they would need to go to Baden to take the waters. In the end, she went alone and on top of everything else, Wolfgang had to defend himself against scandals about alleged lovers who hung around his wife at the health resort. Meanwhile, *The Marriage of Figaro* was revived at the Viennese theatres, and the renewed success stimulated the Emperor to commission a new opera from Mozart. It was 1789 and da Ponte immediately set to work to produce an amusing new libretto out of which came the beautiful opera *Cosi fan Tutte,* which was first performed on January 29, 1790.

The librettist of The Magic Flute *was Emanuel Schikaneder, Director of the Freihaustheater in Wieden, a Viennese suburb. He also sang the role of Papageno. Below: the summer-house which was placed at Mozart's disposal while he was writing the opera, today transferred to the outskirts of the forest at Kapuzinerberg overlooking*

Salzburg. Centre: title page of the 1795 edition of La Clemenza di Tito *and, beside it, a print showing the fire scene in the opera. Bottom: Sanquirico's set for one of the first productions of the opera at La Scala. The first performance in Prague on September 6, 1791, was a Royal gala occasion, but it was not a great success.*

HE CREATED HIS LAST WORKS IN THE MIDST OF ILLNESS AND WORRY

Joseph II died in 1790 and was succeeded by his brother Leopold I, who cared little for Mozart's music or his needs. All the important musicians, including Salieri, were invited to accompany him to Frankfurt for his coronation, but Mozart was ignored. However, Mozart decided he must appear on this occasion and he pawned some silver in order to cover the cost of the journey to Frankfurt. If any concerts were to be given, he must make contact with the musical circles in Frankfurt, and he renewed his acquaintance with the Hatzfield and Scheizer families. He had to wait until after the coronation ceremonies were over to give his concert, which was the least favourable time because the visitors were beginning to leave. However, he played the piano concerto which was later called the *Coronation Concerto* and it was a great success but brought little money. Soon after, Mozart returned to Vienna. It was now winter and on Puchberg's advice he moved from his cold, uncomfortable house on the outskirts back to the centre of the town, hoping this might bring him more pupils: but there were only two. Was it that Mozart was ignored or was it that he had avoided a society of which he no longer felt a part? We owe it to the impresario Emanuel Schikaneder that Mozart was able to write yet another great masterpiece, *The Magic Flute*. He wanted a new opera for his theatre Auf der Wieden and thought of Mozart, who was an old Salzburg acquaintance. Mozart accepted and was at once paid 100 ducats on account. Schikaneder even provided Mozart with a small wooden summer house in the garden near the theatre. Meanwhile another opera commission arrived from Prague. This was for *La Clemenza di Tito,* based on a libretto by Metastasio, and Mozart took only 18 days to compose it, interrupting his work on *The Magic Flute* to do so. It was composed to celebrate the coronation of the king. *La Clemenza di Tito* was performed in Prague on September 6, 1791, but met with a mixed reception from both public and critics. Mozart, however, received his usual warm welcome from the Bohemians. It was noted that his face was pale and anxious and that he frequently had to take medicine. Tired and in poor health, he returned to Vienna to finish *The Magic Flute*.

*Below: Mozart and Cavalieri from
a print in the Museo Teatrale alla
Scala, Milan. Caterina Cavalieri
(1761–1801) was one of the most
notable interpreters of Mozart's
operas. It was she who created
the part of Constanze in* Die
Entführung aus dem Serail, *based
on a libretto by Gottlieb Stephan.
The administrator of the
Burgtheater, Vienna, Stephan,
suggested C. F. Bretzner's comedy
for Mozart's* opera buffa *which
was first performed on July 16,
1782. The singer Cavalieri was the
first interpreter of the part of
Silberklang in* The Impresario,
*first performed at Schönbrunn in
February, 1786. Left: Mozart's
room at Kahlenberg, near Vienna.*

The Magic Flute *reflects Mozart's moral and spiritual belief in man's slow but gradual ascent towards the light. The public were at first puzzled by the nature of the libretto but then the greatness of the opera impressed itself upon them and it received one hundred performances.*

"It is enough that people enjoy the sight of the spectacle—in time its true significance will not fail to be understood," wrote Goethe of the work. Right: a scene from the production of The Magic Flute *at La Scala. Below: a print of 1791 showing Pamina listening to Tamino playing the flute. (Museen der Stadt, Vienna). Bottom: two sets used at the Paris Opéra.*

A PRESAGE OF DEATH IN THE UNFINISHED "REQUIEM"

Mozart fell ill on November 20, 1791, and followed the performance of The Magic Flute *only in his thoughts. He asked some of his intimate friends to come and play him parts of the* Requiem *which he had been able to finish. Below: the dying Mozart conducting a group of singers. (Museo Teatrale alla Scala, Milan).*

A few days after the birth of his last child, Mozart received a strange visitor who left a great impression on him. A thin, pale man, dressed in black and with a sad mysterious demeanour, brought an unsigned letter from someone who wished to remain anonymous, asking him to compose a requiem mass. The messenger brought 100 scùdi on account. When Mozart, Constanze and Sussmayer were in the carriage on their way to Prague for *La Clemenza di Tito,* the mysterious stranger reappeared and, taking Constanze's arm, asked how the requiem was progressing. Mozart was very upset by this, almost believing that the man might be the messenger of death. In fact he was secretary to the Count of Walsegg whose wife had recently died and who wanted to play a requiem for her, but to pass it off as his own work. It was at this time that Lorenzo da Ponte suggested to Wolfgang that they should go on a concert tour to London. Mozart, not feeling in good health, asked for time and finally wrote this letter, in Italian, to da Ponte, which is a pathetic farewell, almost a testament: ". . . I am on the point of expiring. My end has come before

I was able to profit by my talent. And yet life has been so beautiful; my career began under such fortunate auspices. But no-one can change his fate. No-one can count his days; one must resign oneself. What providence determines will be done . . ." This short letter, dated September 7, 1791, affirms how noble was Wolfgang's spirit: notwithstanding his poor health, his debts, his neglect, he could still write: "life has been so beautiful". In November, Constanze was called back to Vienna from Baden. Wolfgang had suffered from fainting fits which drained him of energy, and then was incapacitated by fever. He continued work on the requiem and was even well enough to conduct a performance of his *Little Masonic Cantata* for the Lodge. On the evening of November 19 while with some friends at an Inn, the "Silver Serpent", he was taken very ill. The doctors diagnosed "acute miliary fever". During his delirium it seemed that Mozart was heard to murmur: "Salieri has poisoned me", but this can be seen as true only in the sense that Salieri was a hostile and unhelpful rival.

Mozart's youngest son at the age of 34 (right). Born shortly before Mozart died, he inherited some of his father's musical talent and lived and taught in Salzburg where he died in 1844. His other son Charles (far right—a portrait of about 1840), worked for the Austrian government and died in Milan in 1858. Bottom left:

A. Vigneron's famous painting, The Pauper's Funeral, *which belonged to Beethoven and records Mozart's sad funeral. Bottom right: The room on the first floor of number 970 Rauhensteingasse, where Mozart died. He had lived there since 1790. Below: Mozart's last moments; a print in the Museo Teatrale alla Scala.*

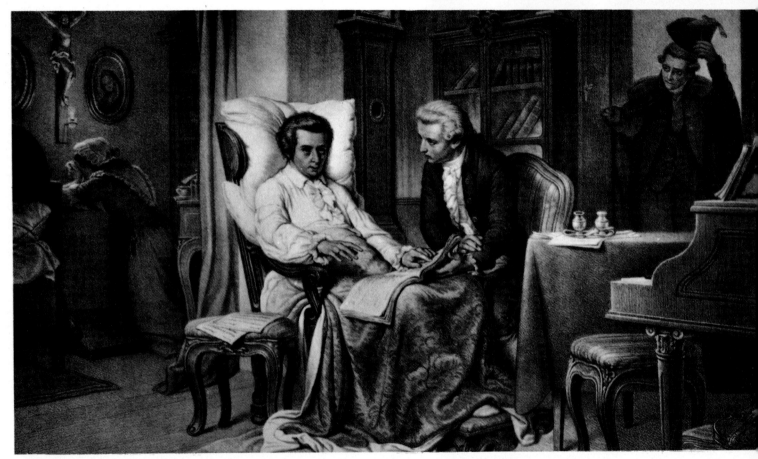

A PAUPER'S FUNERAL AND AN UNKNOWN GRAVE

Ludwig von Köchel (bottom right) compiled a thematic catalogue of Mozart's entire works and it is his initial K which is used in the classification numbers which identify all Mozart's works. The first edition was published in Salzburg in 1862 and was revised by Paul von Waldresse in 1905. However, it is the work of the great scholar Alfred Einstein who devoted his life between 1930–47 to a study of Mozart, which has done most for students of Mozart. Below: the title page of the first Leipzig edition of the Mozart biography written by G. N. von Nissen, Constanze's second husband. Bottom left: a miniature of Constanze in 1826.

On December 4, 1791, after seeing a priest, Mozart gave instructions to Sussmayer, explaining to him the outline of the *Requiem* and still unfinished parts. During the course of the night he lost consciousness and died at about 1 o'clock on the morning of the 5th. He was 35. The doctor had been called but was at the theatre and did not come until it was too late. At the moment of Wolfgang's passing, Constanze and Sussmayer were at his side. Early the next morning, the body was wrapped in a black shroud and placed on a bier in his study beside the piano. Almost as soon as he had died, his death mask was taken. Constanze was quite beside herself with grief and the children were taken away. A cheap funeral was ordered and a few people, amongst whom was Salieri, followed the hearse to St. Steven's church for the funeral service. It is said that there was a snowstorm that day and by the time the funeral carriage reached the cemetery the few friends had dispersed, leaving none to see exactly where the body was placed. However, recent research into contemporary manuscripts has revealed that on December 6, 1791, there was only a little mist in Vienna. Was Mozart really poisoned? According to some theories, it was possible that in an atmosphere overshadowed by the French revolution, with the reactionary bigotry of Leopold II, Mozart, a freemason, who had shown little respect towards the Court, might have provoked enough animosity to inspire someone to eliminate him. But most modern opinion counts the story as idle gossip. It seems probable that Mozart died of Bright's disease, a kidney ailment, aggravated by exhaustion and depression. Meanwhile, his pupil Sussmayer finished the *Requiem* and it was first performed under the name of Walsegg, who had ordered and paid for it. Later, under Wolfgang Amadeus Mozart's own name, it was heard in its true glory at the funerals of Napoleon and Chopin. Later, Mozart's wax death mask was accidentally smashed one day by Constanze while she was cleaning. Now nothing was left of Mozart's body, buried in an unknown grave; all was gone. Constanze herself for some reason did not visit the supposed site of the grave until 1808. But although he died in poverty and disappointment, the music he left is some of the greatest ever written.

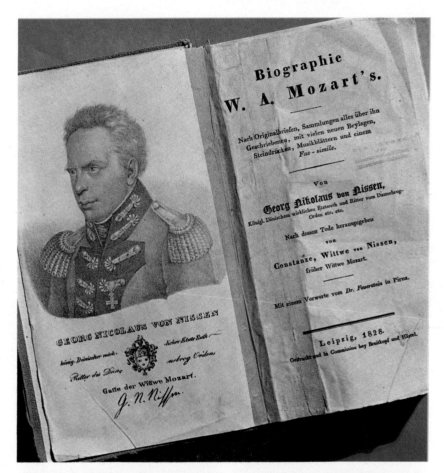

HIS MEMORY LIVES ON IN SALZBURG

They say only those who know Salzburg can understand the full depth of Mozart's music and personality. If, as Paumgartner says, the country is the man, never was a saying truer for Mozart and Salzburg. Though scorned and ignored, nothing diminished his nostalgia for the sky and atmosphere of that town, which did not understand him and abandoned him to his fate. Today, Salzburg cherishes Mozart's memory: it is everywhere apparent—even on tins and chocolate boxes. At the yearly Mozart festival Mozart at last receives the admiration and popularity which eluded him during his lifetime.

Mozart was a poor administrator as far as his own affairs were concerned and did nothing to make himself better understood by his fellow men. He was not equipped to deal with the mundane affairs of daily life: his genius and inspiration were often beyond the comprehension of his contemporaries. Even in music which was simply commissioned for dances or other entertainments his instinct led him to create works which were exceptional. He brought to perfection the art of the concerto form, gave new dimensions of expression to chamber music and symphonic works and was an innovator in the theatre. During the 35 years of his short life, he left us nearly 700 compositions. Their extraordinary originality marks Mozart out as a genius. His music pointed to and anticipated the future and gave impetus and expression to the developments of the 19th century. "People err who think that my art has come easily to me," Mozart is related to have told a friend. "I assure you . . . nobody has devoted so much time and thought to composition as I have." Paradoxically, one of the major impressions his works give is that of spontaneity, despite their strictness of form. They reflect Mozart's enormous vitality, his humour and his complete dedication to music.

1756– January 27: Wolfgang Amadeus Mozart, son of Leopold and Anna Maria Pertle, born at Salzburg.

1762– Mozart wrote his first minuet and an *Allegro in B flat*. In the same year he began his first music tour accompanied by his father and sister and played in the presence of Francis I and Maria Theresa of Austria.

1763– On their second tour they visited several German towns and then Paris, where they stayed for five months.

1764-5– In London they played for George III. He composed his first symphony at Chelsea and the second, in which one hears the influence of Johann Christoph Bach, some months later in London.

1767– After a visit to Holland and a long delay caused by the serious illness of Wolfgang and his sister Marianne, the two young musicians were again in Salzburg. Here Mozart composed the oratorio *The Obligation of the First Commandment*.

1768– He wrote a Mass and his first "opera buffa" *La Finta Semplice*.

1769-71– Mozart's first visit to Italy.

1770– At Bologna he met Padre Giovanni Batista Martini who gave him lessons in counterpoint and encouraged his nomination to membership of the city's Accademia Filarmonica. His first "opera seria" *Mitridate Re di Ponto* was performed in Milan with great success. At Bonn, Ludwig van Beethoven was born.

1771– In August they are again in Italy where *Ascanio in Alba* (libretto by Giuseppe Parini) was produced in Milan.

1774– He composed his opera *La Finta Giardiniera* in Munich for the city's court theatre.

1775– Death of Maestro Giovan Battista Samartini, one of the "fathers" of the symphony, whom Mozart met in Milan.

1777– September: embittered by the behaviour of the new Prince-Archbishop, Count Colloredo, successor to his patron Archbishop Sigismund von Schrattenbach, Mozart left Salzburg accompanied by his mother. After brief visits to Munich, Augsburg and Mannheim, they arrived in Paris. Here during the year that followed he composed the *Symphony in D, The Paris Symphony*.

1778– July 3: His mother dies. September: return to Salzburg.

1779– After his final breach with the Archbishop of Salzburg, he establishes himself in Vienna.

1782– August 4: He marries Constanze Weber, sister of Aloysia with whom he had been in love some years before, at Mannheim. In his opera *Die Entführung aus dem Serail*, which he dedicated to her, the heroine is called Constanze. Death of Metastasio, to whose libretto Mozart composed *Betulia Liberata* (1771) and was to compose *La Clemenza di Tito* 20 years later.

1782-5 He worked particularly on instrumental music (*Haffner* and *Linz Symphonies* and *Six Quartets*, dedicated to Haydn with whom he had deep links of friendship).

1786– May 1: the premier of *The Marriage of Figaro* produced with triumphant success at Vienna and Prague.

1787– May 28: His father dies. Following the success of *The Marriage of Figaro*, the director of the Prague Theatre, Pasquale Bondini, commissioned from Mozart a new opera: thus was written *Don Giovanni*, which received its first performance on October 29, in Prague. On returning to Vienna, the Emperor Joseph II nominated him "Kammermusicus".

1788– He wrote his last three symphonies: the *E flat, G minor* and *C major* (the *Jupiter*).

1789– April 8: He left Vienna with his pupil Prince Karl Lichnowsky for a trip to Germany; however, the hoped-for offers of work from King Frederick William II of Prussia did not materialise and he had to return to Vienna where Joseph II commissioned him to write a new opera, *Cosi fan tutte*.

1790– Death of Joseph II. He was succeeded by Leopold II who did not show his brother's interest in music.

1791– July: Began the composition of the *Requiem*. The work was left incomplete at the composer's death and was finished by his pupil Süssmayer. September 6: *La Clemenza di Tito* performed in Prague. September 30: *The Magic Flute* triumphantly received in Vienna. November 18: The Cantata *Neugekrönte Hoffnung* was Mozart's last complete work. On the night of December 4, he died in Vienna, only 35 years old.

The works reproduced in this volume belong to the following collections: Augsburg, Augsburg State Collection: pp. 4-5. Bologna, Philharmonic Academy: p. 39; School of Music: p. 49. Dusseldorf, Goethe Museum: pp. 18-19, 49. London, British Museum: pp. 20, 22, 23, 25, 29; Royal Academy of Art: p. 24; John Soane Museum: p. 24; Victoria and Albert Museum: pp. 22-23, 23. Milan, Bertarelli Collection: pp. 15, 18, 31, 34, 35, 37, 39, 40, 54, 61, 63; Museum of Musical Instruments: p. 35; pp. 56, 57, 63, 64, 65, 68, 70, 71, 72. Paris, Bibliothèque de l'Opéra: pp. 63, 70; Bibliothèque Nationale: pp. 18, 19, 21, 27, 29, 31, 35, 38, 39, 44, 45, 46, 50, 51, 54, 61, 66; private collection: p. 21; Louvre: end papers, pp. 26-27, 41; Carnavalet Museum: pp. 50-51. Rome, Gallery of Ancient and Modern Art: pp. 36-37. Salzburg, Mozarteum: frontispiece, pp. 5, 7, 8, 10, 11, 12, 17, 18, 28, 30, 33, 34, 35, 38, 40, 43, 44, 44-45, 49, 53, 54, 57, 58, 60, 61, 64, 65, 66, 67, 68, 72, 73; Charles Augustus Museum: pp. 7, 10, 25, 32, 46, 47. Versailles, Museum: p. 21. Vienna, Schönbrunn Castle: p. 14; Austrian National Library: pp. 14, 15, 16, 31, 38, 42, 42-43, 58, 59, 63, 70. Photographic references: Sergio Del Grande: pp. 18-19, 49. Fotolabor: pp. 4-5. John Freeman: pp. 20, 22, 22-23, 23, 24, 25, 29, Agostino Ghilardi: pp. 36-37. Giraudon: end papers, pp. 16, 21, 26-27, 41. Magnum: pp. 6, 15. Erwin Meyer: pp. 42-43, 63, 70. Giorgio Nimatallah: frontispiece, pp. 5, 7, 8, 9, 10, 11, 12, 17, 18, 25, 28, 30, 32, 33, 38, 40, 43, 44, 44-45, 46, 47, 49, 54, 57, 58, 61, 64, 65, 66, 67, 68, 72, 73, 74. Alfredo Panicucci: pp. 13, 14, 17, 48, 53, 54, 56, 59, 61, 62. Erio Piccagliani: p. 64. Pospech: pp. 6, 13, 52, 53. Saporetti: pp. 15, 18, 31, 34, 35, 37, 39, 40, 54, 61, 63. Scala: p. 49. Antonio Scarnati: pp. 18, 19, 21, 27, 29, 31, 35, 38, 39, 44, 45, 46, 50-51, 54, 61, 63, 66, 70; and the Mondadori photographic archives.

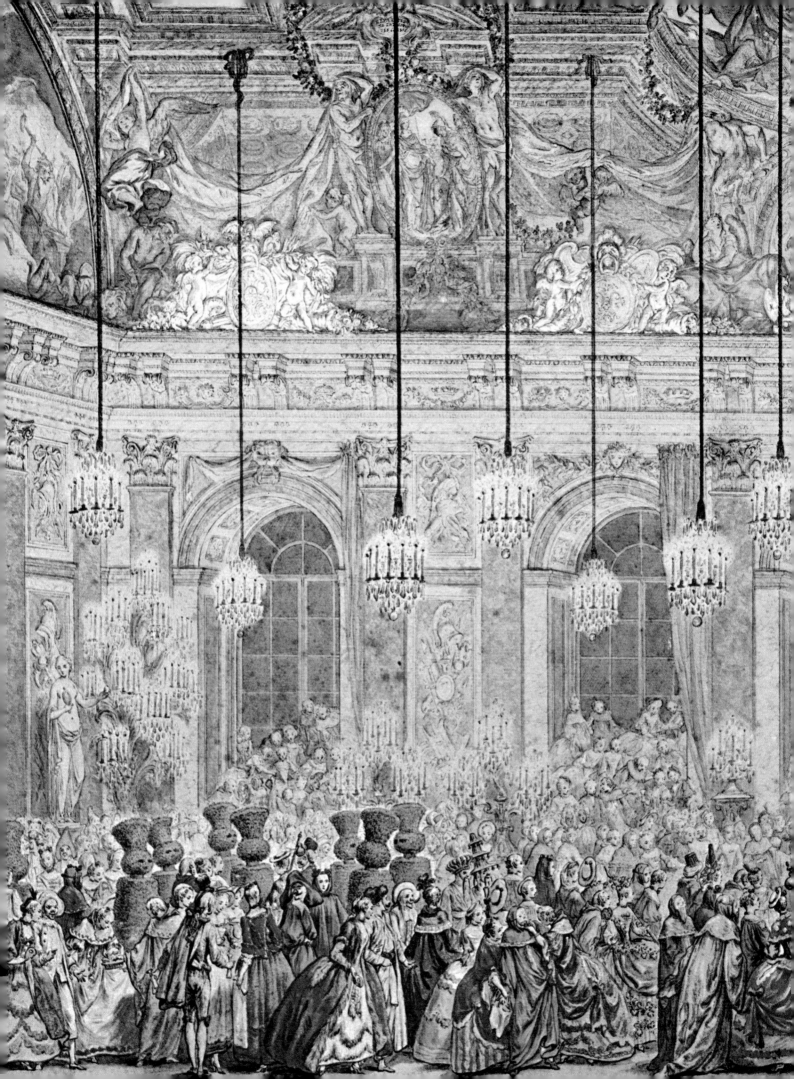